RELIGIONS, VALUES,
AND PEAK-EXPERIENCES

RELIGIONS, VALUES, AND PEAK-EXPERIENCES

BY

ABRAHAM H. MASLOW

THE VIKING PRESS   NEW YORK

This essay is dedicated to

ANDY AND MARY KAY

Viking Compass Edition
Issued in 1970 by The Viking Press, Inc.
625 Madison Avenue, New York, N.Y. 10022

Distributed in Canada by
The Macmillan Company of Canada Limited

SBN 670-00304-2

Published by arrangement with Kappa Delta Pi

Printed in U.S.A.

Sixth printing June 1973

❧ EDITORIAL INTRODUCTION ❧

The world has seen increased communication among political and economic philosophies, among the social sciences, among religions, among the physical sciences, and among people in general. Although there are individual differences in the cultural and material developments of the nations of the world, there has been a growing movement toward the establishment of a world philosophy in the social and physical sciences.

Concurrently with this growth of international communication and the unity it has brought about in the sciences, and the lesser amount of agreement it has engendered among political and social theorists, there has been a rising sentiment in favor of increased communication among, if not unity of, the religions of the world. Protestant groups have abandoned, or are abandoning, their strict sectarian views. The Ecumenical Council has brought changes that, although so far largely procedural, give promise of increased world co-operation between the Roman Catholic church and other faiths. And efforts have been and are being made to reconcile the views of the great religious leaders of all major religions—Jewish, Christian, Muslim, Buddhist, and Hindu—religions that, in the past, have been regarded by their followers as having been founded upon the direct revelation of a supreme being to a chosen earthly prophet.

Traditionally, religion has been of the spirit; science, of the body; and there has been a wide philosophic gulf between the knowledge of body and the knowledge of spirit. The natural sciences and religion have generally been considered as natural and eternal opponents.

William James, through his psychology, especially his *Varieties of Religious Experience,* and John Dewey, in his *A Common Faith,* have strongly influenced the views of Dr. Maslow in this, the thirty-fifth volume in the "Kappa Delta Pi Lecture Series." Dissenting from the followers of those prophets who claimed direct revelation from God, and from the nineteenth-century scientists who denied not only direct revelation but God himself, the author declares that these revelations were, in his words, "peak-experiences" which are characteristic not only of specially ordained emissaries of God but of mankind in general. Dr. Maslow considers these revelations valid psychological events worthy of scientific, rather than metaphysical, study —keys to a better understanding of a peculiarly "human" aspect of man's existence.

This volume is presented as a contribution to philosophical and scientific thinking, as one interpretation of a fundamental aspect of life, as a step toward a better understanding among the religions of the world, and as a possible program for the development of a healthy relationship between modern science and modern theology.

E. I. F. Williams, Editor
Kappa Delta Pi Publications

❧ PREFACE ❧

Since this book was first written, there has been much turmoil in the world and, therefore, much to learn. Several of the lessons I have learned are relevant here, certainly in the sense that they are helpful supplements to the main thesis of the book. Or perhaps I should call them warnings about over-extreme, dangerous, and one-sided *uses* of this thesis. Of course, this is a standard hazard for thinkers who try to be holistic, integrative, and inclusive. They learn inevitably that most people think atomistically, in terms of either-or, black-white, all in or all out, of mutual exclusiveness and separativeness. A good example of what I mean is the mother who gave her son two ties for his birthday. As he put on one of them to please her, she asked sadly, "And why do you hate the other tie?"

I think I can best state my warning against polarization and dichotomizing by a historical approach. I see in the history of many organized religions a tendency to develop two extreme wings: the "mystical" and individual on the one hand, and the legalistic and organizational on the other. The profoundly and authentically religious person integrates these trends easily and automatically. The forms, rituals, ceremonials, and verbal formulae in which he was reared remain for him experientially rooted, symbolically meaningful, archetypal, unitive. Such a person may go through the same motions and behaviors as his more numerous co-religionists, but he is never *reduced* to the behavioral, as most of them are. Most people lose or forget the subjectively religious experience, and redefine Religion[1] as a set of habits, behaviors, dogmas, forms, which at the extreme becomes entirely legalistic and bureaucratic, conventional, empty, and in the truest meaning of the word, anti-religious. The mystic experience, the illumination, the great awakening, along with the charismatic seer who started the whole thing, are forgotten, lost, or transformed into their opposites. Organized Religion, the churches, finally may become the major enemies of the religious experience and the religious experiencer. This is a main thesis of this book.

But on the other wing, the mystical (or experiential) also has its traps which I have not stressed sufficiently. As the more Apollonian type can veer toward the extreme of being reduced to the merely behavioral, so does the mystical type run the risk of being reduced to the merely experiential. Out of the joy and wonder of his ecstasies and peak-experiences he may be tempted to *seek* them, *ad hoc*, and to value them exclusively, as the only or at least the highest goods of life, giving up other criteria of right and wrong. Focused on these wonderful subjective experiences, he may run the danger of turning away from the world and from other people in his search for triggers to peak-experiences, *any* triggers. In a word, instead of being temporarily self-absorbed and inwardly searching, he may become simply a selfish person, seeking his own personal salvation, trying

[1] I have found it useful to differentiate the subjective and naturalistic religious experience and attitude from the institutionalized, conventional, organized Religions by using lower case for the former (calling it "small r religion") and capitalizing the R in "big R Religion."

to get into "heaven" even if other people can't, and finally even perhaps *using* other people as triggers, as means to his sole end of higher states of consciousness. In a word, he may become not only selfish but also evil. My impression, from the history of mysticism, is that this trend can sometimes wind up in meanness, nastiness, loss of compassion, or even in the extreme of sadism.

Another possible booby trap for the (polarizing) mystics throughout history has been the danger of needing to escalate the triggers, so to speak. That is, stronger and stronger stimuli are needed to produce the same response. If the *sole* good in life becomes the peak-experience, and if all means to this end become good, and if more peak-experiences are better than fewer, then one can *force* the issue, push actively, strive and hunt and fight for them. So they have often moved over into magic, into the secret and esoteric, into the exotic, the occult, the dramatic and effortful, the dangerous, the cultish. Healthy openness to the mysterious, the realistically humble recognition that we don't know much, the modest and grateful acceptance of gratuitous grace and of just plain good luck—all these can shade over into the anti-rational, the anti-empirical, the anti-scientific, the anti-verbal, the anti-conceptual. The peak-experience may then be exalted as the best or even the *only* path to knowledge, and thereby all the tests and verifications of the *validity* of the illumination may be tossed aside.

The possibility that the inner voices, the "revelations," may be mistaken, a lesson from history that should come through loud and clear, is denied, and there is then no way of finding out whether the voices within are the voices of good or evil. (George Bernard Shaw's *Saint Joan* confronts this problem.) Spontaneity (the impulses from our best self) gets confused with impulsivity and acting out (the impulses from our sick self), and there is then no way to tell the difference.

Impatience (especially the built-in impatience of youth) dictates shortcuts of all kinds. Drugs, which can be helpful when wisely used, become dangerous when foolishly used. The sudden insight becomes "all," and the patient and disciplined "working through" is postponed or devalued. Instead of being "surprised by joy," "turning on" is scheduled, promised, advertised, sold, hustled into being, and can get to be regarded as a commodity. Sex-love, certainly one possible path to the experience of the sacred, can become mere "screwing," i.e., desacralized. More and more exotic, artificial, striving "techniques" may escalate further and further until they become *necessary* and until jadedness and impotence ensue.

The search for the exotic, the strange, the unusual, the uncommon has often taken the form of pilgrimages, of turning away from the world, the "Journey to the East," to another country or to a different Religion. The great lesson from the true mystics, from the Zen monks, and now also from the Humanistic and Transpersonal psychologists— that the sacred is *in* the ordinary, that it is to be found in one's daily life, in one's neighbors, friends, and family, in one's back yard, and that travel may be a *flight* from confronting the sacred—this lesson can be easily lost. To be looking elsewhere for miracles is to me a sure sign of ignorance that *everything* is miraculous.

The rejection of a priestly caste who claimed to be exclusive custodians of a private hot line to the sacred was, in my opinion, a great step forward in the emancipation of mankind, and we have the mystics—among others—to thank for this achievement. But this valid insight can also be used badly when dichotomized and exaggerated by foolish people. They can distort it into a rejection of the guide, the teacher, the sage, the therapist, the counselor, the elder, the helper along the path to self-actualization and the realm of Being. This is often a great danger and always an unnecessary handicap.

To summarize, the healthily Apollonian (which means integrated with the healthily Dionysian) can become pathologized into an extreme, exaggerated, and dichotomized compulsive-obsessional sickness. But also the healthily Dionysian (which means integrated with the healthily Apollonian) can become pathologized at its extreme into hysteria with all *its* symptoms.[1]

Obviously, what I am suggesting here is a pervasively holistic attitude and way of thinking. Not only must the experimental be stressed and brought back into psychology and philosophy as an *opponent* of the merely abstract and abstruse, of the a priori, of what I have called "helium-filled words." It must then also be *integrated* with the abstract and the verbal, i.e., we must make a place for "experien-

---

[1] Colin Wilson's "Outsider" series will furnish all the examples necessary.

tially based concepts," and for "experientially filled words," that is, for an experience-based rationality in contrast to the a priori rationality that we have come almost to identify with rationality itself.

The same sort of thing is true for the relations between experientialism and social reform. Shortsighted people make them opposites, mutually exclusive. Of course, historically this has often happened and does today still happen in many. But it need not happen. It is a mistake, an atomistic error, an example of the dichotomizing and pathologizing that goes along with immaturity. The empirical fact is that self-actualizing people, our best experiencers, are also our most compassionate, our great improvers and reformers of society, our most *effective* fighters against injustice, inequality, slavery, cruelty, exploitation (and also our best fighters *for* excellence, effectiveness, competence). And it also becomes clearer and clearer that the best "helpers" are the most fully human persons. What I may call the bodhisattvic path is an *integration* of self-improvement and social zeal, i.e., the best way to become a better "helper" is to become a better person. But one necessary aspect of becoming a better person is *via* helping other people. So one must and can do both simultaneously. (The question "Which comes first" is an atomistic question.)

In this context I would like to refer to my demonstration in the Preface to the revised edition (1970) of my *Motivation and Personality* (59)[1] that normative zeal is *not* incompatible with scientific objectivity, but can be integrated

[1] Numbers in parentheses refer to items in the Bibliography.

with it, eventuating in a higher form of objectivity, i.e., the Taoistic.

What this all adds up to is this: small r religion is quite compatible, at the higher levels of personal development, with rationality, with science, with social passion. Not only this, but it can, in principle, quite easily integrate the healthily animal, material, and selfish with the naturalistically transcendent, spiritual, and axiological. (See my "A Theory of Metamotivation: The Biological Rooting of the Value-Life," *Journal of Humanistic Psychology*, 1967, VII, 93–127.)

For other reasons also, I now consider that the book was too imbalanced toward the individualistic and too hard on groups, organizations, and communities. Even within these last six or seven years we have learned not to think of organizations as *necessarily* bureaucratic, as we have learned more about humanistic, need-fulfilling kinds of groups, from, e.g., the research in Organization Development and Theory Y management, the rapidly accumulating experience with T-groups, encounter groups, and personal-growth groups, the successes of the Synanon community, of the Israeli kibbutzim, etc. (See my listing of the Eupsychian Network, an appendix in the revised edition [1968] of my *Toward a Psychology of Being* [70].)

As a matter of fact, I can say much more firmly than I ever did, for many empirical reasons, that basic human needs can be fulfilled *only* by and through other human beings, i.e., society. The need for community (belongingness, contact, groupiness) is itself a basic need. Loneliness, isolation, ostracism, rejection by the group—these are not only painful but pathogenic as well. And of course it has also been known for decades that humanness and specieshood in the infant are only a potentiality and must be actualized by the society.

My study of the failure of most Utopian efforts has taught me to ask the basic questions themselves in a more practicable and researchable way. "How good a society does human nature permit?" and, "How good a human nature does society permit?" (For the implications of this way of asking the questions, see my *Eupsychian Management: A Journal* [1965] [69] and my paper "Some Fundamental Questions that Face the Normative Social Psychologist," *Journal of Humanistic Psychology*, 1968, VIII.)

Finally, I would now add to the peak-experience material a greater consideration, not only of nadir-experiences, the psycholytic therapy of Groff, confrontations with and reprieves from death, postsurgical visions, etc., but also of the "plateau-experience." This is serene and calm, rather than a poignantly emotional, climactic, autonomic response to the miraculous, the awesome, the sacralized, the Unitive, the B-values. So far as I can now tell, the high plateau-experience *always* has a noetic and cognitive element, which is not always true for peak-experiences, which can be purely and exclusively emotional. It is far more voluntary than peak-experiences are. One can learn to see in this Unitive way almost at will. It then becomes a witnessing, an appreciating, what one might call a serene, cognitive blissfulness which can, however, have a quality of casualness and of lounging about.

There is more an element of surprise, and of disbelief, and of esthetic shock in the peak-experience, more the quality of having such an experience for the *first time*. I have pointed out elsewhere that the aging body and nervous system is less capable of tolerating a really shaking peak-experience. I would add here that maturing and aging mean also some loss of first-timeness, of novelty, of sheer unpreparedness and surprise.

Peak- and plateau-experience differ also in their relations to death. The peak-experience itself can often meaningfully be called a "little death," and a rebirth in various senses. The less intense plateau-experience is more often experienced as pure enjoyment and happiness, as, let's say, in a mother sitting quietly looking, by the hour, at her baby playing, and marveling, wondering, philosophizing, not quite believing. She can experience this as a very pleasant, continuing, contemplative experience rather than as something akin to a climactic explosion which then ends.

Older people, making their peace with death, are more apt to be profoundly touched with (sweet) sadness and tears at the contrast between their own mortality and the eternal quality of what sets off the experience. This contrast can make far more poignant and precious what is being witnessed, e.g., "The surf will be here forever and you will soon be gone. So hang on to it, appreciate it, be fully conscious of it. Be grateful for it. You are lucky."

Very important today in a topical sense is the realization that plateau-experiencing can be achieved, learned, earned by long hard work. It can be meaningfully aspired to. But I don't know of any way of bypassing the necessary maturing, experiencing, living, learning. All of this takes time. A transient glimpse is certainly possible in the peak-experiences which may, after all, come sometimes to anyone. But, so to speak, to take up residence on the high plateau of Unitive consciousness—that is another matter altogether. That tends to be a lifelong effort. It should not be confused with the Thursday-evening turn-on that many youngsters think of as *the* path to transcendence. For that matter, it should not be confused with *any* single experience. The "spiritual disciplines," both the classical ones and the new ones that keep on being discovered these days, all take time, work, discipline, study, commitment.

There is much more to say about these states which are clearly relevant to the life of transcendence and the transpersonal, and to experiencing life at the level of Being. All I wish to do here with this brief mention is to correct the tendency of some to identify experiences of transcendence as *only* dramatic, orgasmic, transient, "peaky," like a moment on the top of Mount Everest. There is also the high plateau, where one can *stay* "turned on."

If I were to summarize both the book and my remarks in this Preface in a few words, I would say it this way: Man has a higher and transcendent nature, and this is part of his essence, i.e., his biological nature as a member of a species which has evolved. This means to me something which I had better spell out clearly, namely, that this is a flat rejection of the Sartre type of Existentialism, i.e., its denial of species-hood, and of a biological human nature, and its refusal to face the existence of the biological sciences. It is true that the word *Existentialism* is by now used in so many different ways by different people, even in contradictory ways, that this indictment does not apply to all who use the label. But just *because* of this diversity of usage, the word is now almost useless, in my opinion, and had better be dropped. The trouble is that I have no good alternative label to offer. If only there were some way to say simultaneously: "Yes, man is in a way his own project and he does make himself. But also there are limits upon what he can make himself into. The 'project' is predetermined biologically for all men; it is to become a man. He cannot adopt as his project for himself to become a chimpanzee. Or even a female. Or a baby." The right label would have to combine the humanistic, the transpersonal, and the transhuman. Besides, it would have to be experiential (phenomenological), at least in its basing. It would have to be holistic rather than dissecting. And it would have to be empirical rather than a priori, etc., etc.

The reader who is especially interested in continuing developments along the lines of this book may be referred to the recently established (1969) *Journal of Transpersonal Psychology* (P. O. Box 4437, Stanford, California 94305), and to the older weekly, *Manas* (P. O. Box 32112, El Sereno Station, Los Angeles, California 90032).

Dr. Abraham H. Maslow
The W. P. Laughlin Charitable Foundation
1 Saga Lane
Menlo Park, California 94025
May, 1970

❦ CONTENTS ❦

RELIGIONS, VALUES,
AND PEAK-EXPERIENCES

INTRODUCTION

Some time ago, after the Supreme Court decision on prayer in the public schools, a so-called patriotic women's organization—I forget which one—bitterly attacked the decision as antireligious. They were in favor of "spiritual values," they said, whereas the Supreme Court was destroying them.

I am very much in favor of a clear separation of church and state, and my reaction was automatic: I disagreed with the women's organization. But then something happened that set me to thinking for many months. It dawned on me that I, too, was in favor of spiritual values and that, indeed, my researches and theoretical investigations had gone far toward demonstrating their reality. I had reacted in an automatic way against the whole statement by the organization, thereby implicitly accepting its erroneous definition and concept of spiritual values. In a word, I had allowed these intellectual primitives to capture a good word and to put *their* peculiar meaning to it, just as they had taken the fine word "patriotic" and contaminated and destroyed it. I had let them redefine these words and had then accepted their definitions. And now I want to take them back. I want to demonstrate that spiritual values have naturalistic meaning, that they are not the exclusive possession of organized churches, that they do not need supernatural concepts to validate them, that they are well within the jurisdiction of a suitably enlarged science, and that, therefore, they are the general responsibility of *all* mankind. If all of this is so, then we shall have to re-evaluate the possible place of spiritual and moral values in education. For, if these values are not exclusively identified with churches, then teaching values in the schools need not breach the wall between church and state.

The Supreme Court decisions on prayer in the public schools were seen (mistakenly, as we shall see) by many Americans as a rejection of spiritual values in education. Much of the turmoil was in defense of these higher values and eternal verities rather than of the prayers as such. That is to say, very many people in our society apparently see organized religion as *the* locus, *the* source, *the* custodian and guardian and teacher of the spiritual life. Its methods, its style of teaching, its content are widely and officially accepted as *the* path, by many as the *only* path, to the life of righteousness, of purity and virtue, of justice and goodness, etc.[1]

---

[1] As a matter of fact, this identity is so profoundly built into the English language that it is almost impossible to speak of the "spiritual life" (a distasteful phrase to a scientist, and especially to a psychologist) without using the vocabulary of traditional religion. There just isn't any other satisfactory language yet. A trip to the thesaurus will demonstrate this very quickly. This makes an almost insoluble problem for the writer who is intent on demonstrating that the common base of all religions is human, natural, empirical, and that so-called spiritual values are also naturally derivable. But I have available only a theistic language for this "scientific" job.

This is also true, paradoxically enough, for many orthodoxly positivistic scientists, philosophers, and other intellectuals. Pious positivists as a group accept the same strict dichotomizing of facts and values that the professional religionists do. Since they exclude values from the realm of science and from the realm of exact, rational, positivistic knowledge, all values are turned over by default to non-scientists and to non-rationalists (i.e., to "non-knowers") to deal with. Values can be arbitrarily affirmed by fiat only, they think, like a taste or a preference or a belief which cannot be scientifically validated, proven, confirmed, or disconfirmed. Therefore, it appears that such scientists and such philosophers really have no argument either for or against the churches; even though, as a group, they are not very likely to respect the churches. (Even this lack of respect is, for them, only a matter of taste and cannot be supported scientifically.)

Something of this sort is certainly true for many psychologists and many educators. It is almost *universally* true for the positivistic psychologists, the behaviorists, the

---

Perhaps I can get out of this terminological difficulty in another way. If you look up the words "sacred," "divine," "holy," "numen," "sin," "prayer," "oblation," "thanksgiving," "worship," "piety," "salvation," "reverence," the dictionary will most often tell you that they refer to a god or to a religion in the supernatural sense. Now what I want to say is that each and all of these words, and many other "religious" words, have been reported to me by non-theistic people in their effort to describe particular subjective happenings in "non-religious" (in the conventional sense) peak-experiences and illuminations. These words are the only words available to describe certain happenings in the natural world. This vocabulary is the language of a theory which people have had about these subjective happenings, a theory which is no longer necessary.

I shall, therefore, use these words, since I have no others to use, to refer to subjective happenings in human beings without necessarily implying any supernatural reference. I claim that it is not necessary to appeal to principles outside of nature and human nature in order to explain these experiences.

5

neo-behaviorists, and the ultra-experimentalists, all of whom feel values and the life of value to be none of their professional concern, and who casually renounce all consideration of poetry and art and of any of the religious or transcendent experiences. Indeed, the pure positivist rejects any inner experiences of *any* kind as being "unscientific," as not in the realm of human knowledge, as not susceptible of study by a scientific method, because such data are not objective, that is to say, public and shared. This is a kind of "reduction to the concrete," to the tangible, the visible, the audible, to that which can be recorded by a machine, to behavior.[2]

The other dominating theory of psychology, the Freudian, coming from a very different compass direction winds up at a similar terminus, denying that it has anything much to do with spiritual or ethical values. Freud himself and H. Hartman (28)[3] after him say something like this: "The only goal of the psychoanalytic method is to undo repressions and all other defenses against seeing unpleasant truth; it has nothing to do with ideologies, indoctrinations, religious dogmas or teaching a way of life or system of values." (Even Alan Wheelis [89], thoughtful and probing though he may be, comes to a similar conclusion.) Observe here the unwitting acceptance of the unexamined

---

[2] This is an especially fantastic notion in the context of this lecture, because human behavior is so often a defense *against* motives, emotions, and impulses. That is, it is a way of inhibiting and concealing them as often as it is an expression of them. Behavior is often a means of *preventing* the overt expression of everything I'm talking about, just as spoken language can also be. How then can we explain the quick spread of that theory-bound, sectarian, question-begging phrase: "The behavorial sciences"? I confess that I cannot.

[3] Numbers in parentheses refer to items in the Bibliography.

belief that values are taught, in the traditional sense of indoctrination, and that they must, therefore, be arbitrary, and also that they really have nothing to do with facts, with truth, with discovery, with uncovering the values and "value-hungers" that lie deeply within human nature itself.

And so official, orthodox, Freudian psychoanalysis remains essentially a system of psychopathology and of cure of psychopathology. It does not supply us with a psychology of the higher life or of the "spiritual life," of what the human being should grow *toward*, of what he can become (although I believe psychoanalytic method and theory is a necessary substructure for any such "higher" or growth psychology [70]). Freud came out of nineteenth-century, mechanistic, physical-chemical, reductionistic science; and there his more Talmudic followers remain, at least with respect to the theory of values and everything that has to do with values. Indeed this reductionism goes so far sometimes that the Freudians seem almost to say that the "higher life" is just a set of "defenses against the instincts," especially denial and reaction-formation. Were it not for the concept of sublimation, that is what they would have to be saying. Unfortunately, sublimation is so weak and unsatisfactory a concept that it simply cannot bear this huge responsibility. Thus, psychoanalysis often comes perilously close to being a nihilistic and value-denying philosophy of man. (It is fortunate that any really good therapist in practice pays no attention to this philosophy. Such a therapist often functions by an unconscious philosophy of man which may not be worked out scientifically for another century. It is true

7

that there are interesting and exciting developments in psychoanalysis today, but they are coming from the unorthodox.) It must be said to Freud's credit that, though he was at his poorest with all the questions of transcendence, he is still to be preferred to the behaviorists who not only have no answers but who also deny the very questions themselves.

Neither are the humanistic scholars and artists of any great help these days. They used to be, and were supposed to be, as a group, carriers of and teachers of the eternal verities and the higher life. The goal of humanistic studies was defined as the perception and knowledge of the good, the beautiful, and the true. Such studies were expected to refine the discrimination between what is excellent and what is not (excellence generally being understood to be the true, the good, and the beautiful). They were supposed to inspire the student to the better life, to the higher life, to goodness and virtue. What was truly valuable, Matthew Arnold said, was "the acquainting ourselves with the best that has been known and said in the world." And no one disagreed with him. Nor did it need to be spelled out that he meant knowledge of the classics; these were the universally accepted models.

But in recent years and to this day, most humanistic scholars and most artists have shared in the general collapse of all traditional values. And when these values collapsed, there were no others readily available as replacements. And so today, a very large proportion of our artists, novelists, dramatists, critics, literary and historical scholars are disheartened or pessimistic or despairing, and

8

a fair proportion are nihilistic or cynical (in the sense of believing that no "good life" is possible and that the so-called higher values are all a fake and a swindle).

Certainly the young student coming to the study of the arts and the humanities will find therein no inspiring certainties. What criterion of selection does he have between, let us say, Tolstoy and Kafka, between Renoir and De-Kooning, or between Brahms and Cage? And which well-known artists or writers today are trying to teach, to inspire, to conduce to virtue? Which of them could even use this word "virtue" without gagging? Upon which of them can an "idealistic" young man model himself?

No, it is quite clear from our experience of the last fifty years or so that the pre-1914 certainties of the humanists, of the artists, of the dramatists and poets, of the philosophers, of the critics, and of those who are generally inner-directed have given way to a chaos of relativism. No one of these people now knows how and what to choose, nor does he know how to defend and to validate his choice. Not even the critics who are fighting nihilism and value-lessness can do much except to attack, as, for instance, Joseph Wood Krutch does (40, 41); and he has nothing very inspiring or affirmative to suggest that we fight *for*, much less die for.

We can no longer rely on tradition, on consensus, on cultural habit, on unanimity of belief to give us our values. These agreed-upon traditions are all gone. Of course, we never *should* have rested on tradition—as its failures must have proven to everyone by now—it never was a firm foundation. It was destroyed too easily by truth, by honesty,

9

by the facts, by science, by simple, pragmatic, historical failure.

Only truth itself can be our foundation, our base for building. Only empirical, naturalistic knowledge, in its broadest sense, can serve us now. I hesitate to use the word "science" here, because this itself is a moot concept; and I shall be suggesting later in this essay an overhauling and redefinition of science that could make it capable of serving better our value purposes, to make it more inclusive and less excluding, more accepting of the world and less snobbish about its jurisdictions. It is in this broader sense, which I shall be sketching out, that science—meaning *all* confirmable knowledge in *all* its stages of development—begins to look capable of handling values.

Especially will our new knowledge of human nature probably give the humanists and the artists, as well as the religionists, the firm criteria of selection, which they now lack, to choose between the many value possibilities which clamor for belief, so many that the chaos may fairly be called valuelessness.

DICHOTOMIZED SCIENCE AND
DICHOTOMIZED RELIGION

My thesis is, in general, that new developments in psychology are forcing a profound change in our philosophy of science, a change so extensive that we may be able to accept the basic religious questions as a proper part of the jurisdiction of science, once science is broadened and redefined.

It is because both science and religion have been too narrowly conceived, and have been too exclusively dichotomized and separated from each other, that they have been seen to be two mutually exclusive worlds. To put it briefly, this separation permitted nineteenth-century science to become too exclusively mechanistic, too positivistic, too reductionistic, too desperately attempting to be value-free. It mistakenly conceived of itself as having nothing to say about ends or ultimate values or spiritual values. This is the same as saying that these ends are entirely outside the range of natural human knowledge, that they can never be known in a confirmable, validated way, in a way that could satisfy intelligent men, as facts satisfy them.

11

Such an attitude dooms science to be nothing more than technology, amoral and non-ethical (as the Nazi doctors taught us). Such a science can be no more than a collection of instrumentalities, methods, techniques, nothing but a tool to be used by any man, good or evil, and for any ends, good or evil (59).

This dichotomizing of knowledge and values has also pathologized the organized religions by cutting them off from facts, from knowledge, from science, even to the point of often making them the enemies of scientific knowledge. In effect, it tempts them to say that they have nothing more to learn.

But something is happening now to both science and religion, at least to their more intelligent and sophisticated representatives. These changes make possible a very different attitude by the less narrow scientist toward the religious questions, at least to the naturalistic, humanistic, religious questions. It might be said that this is simply one more instance of what has happened so often in the past, i.e., of snatching away another territory from the jurisdiction of organized religion.

Just as each science was once a part of the body of organized religion but then broke away to become independent, so also it can be said that the same thing may now be happening to the problems of values, ethics, spirituality, morals. They are being taken away from the exclusive jurisdiction of the institutionalized churches and are becoming the "property," so to speak, of a new type of humanistic scientist who is vigorously denying the old claim of the established religions to be the sole arbiters of all questions of faith and morals.

This relation between religion and science could be stated in such a dichotomous, competitive way, but I think I can show that it need not be, and that the person who is deeply religious—in a particular sense that I shall discuss—must rather feel strengthened and encouraged by the prospect that his value questions may be more firmly answered than ever before.

Sooner or later, we shall have to redefine both religion and science.

As always, dichotomizing pathologizes (and pathology dichotomizes). Isolating two interrelated parts of a whole from each other, parts that need each other, parts that are truly "parts" and not wholes, distorts them both, sickens and contaminates them (54). Ultimately, it even makes them non-viable. An illustration of this point can be found in Philip Wylie's fascinating novel *The Disappearance*. When men and women disappear into two separated, isolated worlds, both sexes become corrupted and pathologized. The point is driven home fully that they need each other in order to be themselves.

When all that could be called "religious" (naturalistically as well as supernaturalistically) was cut away from science, from knowledge, from further discovery, from the possibility of skeptical investigation, from confirming and disconfirming, and, therefore, from the possibility of purifying and improving, such a dichotomized religion was doomed. It tended to claim that the founding revelation was complete, perfect, final, and eternal. It had the truth, the whole truth, and had nothing more to learn, thereby being pushed into the position that has destroyed so many

13

churches, of resisting change, of being *only* conservative, of being anti-intellectual and anti-scientific, of making piety and obedience exclusive of skeptical intellectuality— in effect, of contradicting naturalistic truth.

Such a split-off religion generates split-off and partial definition of all necessary concepts. For example, faith, which has perfectly respectable naturalistic meanings, as for example in Fromm's writings, tends in the hands of an anti-intellectual church to degenerate into blind belief, sometimes even "belief in what you know ain't so." It tends to become unquestioning obedience and last-ditch loyalty no matter what. It tends to produce sheep rather than men. It tends to become arbitrary and authoritarian (46).

The word "sacred" is another instance of the pathologizing by isolation and by splitting-off. If the sacred becomes the exclusive jurisdiction of a priesthood, and if its supposed validity rests only upon supernatural foundations, then, in effect, it is taken out of the world of nature and of human nature. It is dichotomized sharply from the profane or secular and begins to have nothing to do with them, or even becomes their contradictory. It becomes associated with particular rites and ceremonies, with a particular day of the week, with a particular building, with a particular language, even with a particular musical instrument or certain foods. It does not infuse all of life but becomes compartmentalized. It is not the property then of all men, but only of some. It is no longer ever-present as a possibility in the everyday affairs of men but becomes instead a museum piece without daily usefulness; in effect, such a religion must separate the actual from the ideal and

14

rupture the necessary dynamic interplay between them. The dialectic between them, the mutual effect and feedback, the constant shaping of each other, their usefulness to each other, even, I would say, their absolute need for each other is disrupted and made impossible of fulfillment. What happens then? We have seen often enough throughout history the church whose pieties are mouthed in the middle of human exploitation and degradation as if the one had nothing to do with the other ("Render unto Caesar that which is Caesar's"). This pie-in-the-sky kind of religion, which often enough has turned into an actual *support* of daily evil, is almost inevitable when the existent has no intrinsic and constant connection with the ideal, when heaven is off some place far away from the earth, when human improvement becomes impossible *in* the world but can be achieved only by renouncing the world. "For endeavor for the better is moved by faith in what is possible, not by adherence to the actual," as John Dewey pointed out. (14, p. 23).

And this brings us to the other half of the dichotomy, dichotomized science. Whatever we may say about split-off religion is very similar or complementary to what we may say of split-off science.

For instance, in the division of the ideal and the actual, dichotomized science claims that it deals only with the actual and the existent and that it has nothing to do with the ideal, that is to say, with the ends, the goals, the purposes of life, i.e., with end-values. Any criticism that could be made of half-religion can equally be made of half-science in a complementary way. For instance, corresponding to the blind religions' "reduction to the abstract" (71)

—its blindness to the raw fact, to the concrete, to living human experience itself—we find in non-aspiring science a "reduction to the concrete," of the kind that Goldstein has described (23, 24), and to the tangible and immediately visible and audible. It becomes amoral, even sometimes anti-moral and even anti-human, merely technology which can be bought by anyone for any purpose, like the German "scientists" who could work with equal zeal for Nazis, for Communists, or for Americans. We have been taught very amply in the last few decades that science can be dangerous to human ends and that scientists can become monsters as long as science is conceived to be akin to a chess game, an end in itself, with arbitrary rules, whose only purpose is to explore the existent, and which then makes the fatal blunder of excluding subjective experience from the realm of the existent or explorable.

So also for the exclusion of the sacred and the transcendent from the jurisdiction of science. This makes impossible in principle the study, for instance, of certain aspects of the abstract: psychotherapy, naturalistic religious experience, creativity, symbolism, play, the theory of love, mystical and peak-experiences, not to mention poetry, art, and a lot more (since these all involve an integration of the realm of Being with the realm of the concrete).

To mention only one example that has to do directly with education, it could be shown easily that the good teacher must have what I have called elsewhere B-love (unselfish love) for the child, what Rogers has called unconditional positive regard (82), and what others have called—meaningfully, I would maintain—the sacredness of each individual. To stigmatize these as "normative" or value-laden and, therefore, as "unscientific" concepts is to make impossible certain necessary researches into the nature of the good teacher.

And so it could go on and on almost indefinitely. I have already written much on scientistic, nineteenth-century, orthodox science, and intend to write more. Here I have been dealing with it from the point of view of the dichotomizing of science and religion, of facts (merely and solely) from values (merely and solely), and have tried to indicate that such a splitting off of mutually exclusive jurisdictions must produce cripple-science and cripple-religion, cripple-facts and cripple-values.

Obviously such a conclusion concerns the spiritual and ethical values that I started with (as well as the needs and hungers for these values). *Very* obviously, such values and such hungers cannot be handed over to any church for safekeeping. They cannot be removed from the realm of human inquiry, of skeptical examination, of empirical investigation. But I have tried to demonstrate that orthodox science neither wants this job nor is able to carry it out. Clearly what is needed then is an expanded science, with larger powers and methods, a science which is able to study values and to teach mankind about them.

Such a science would and—insofar as it already exists— *does* include much that has been called religious. As a matter of fact, this expanded science includes among its concerns practically everything in religion that can bear naturalistic observation.

I think I may go so far as to say that if we were to make a list of the key words which have hitherto been considered

17

to be the property of organized religion and which were considered to be entirely outside the jurisdiction of "science" of the older sort, **we would find** that each and all of these words today are acquiring a perfectly naturalistic meaning, i.e., they are within the jurisdiction of scientific investigation. (See Appendix A.)

Let me try to say it in still another way. One could say that the nineteenth-century atheist had burnt down the house instead of remodeling it. He had thrown out the religious questions with the religious answers, because he had to reject the religious answers. That is, he turned his back on the whole religious enterprise because organized religion presented him with a set of answers which he could not intellectually accept—which rested on no evidence which a self-respecting scientist could swallow. But what the more sophisticated scientist is now in the process of learning is that though he must disagree with most of the answers to the religious questions which have been given by organized religion, it is increasingly clear that the religious questions themselves—and religious quests, the religious yearnings, the religious needs themselves—are perfectly respectable scientifically, that they are rooted deep in human nature, that they can be studied, described, examined in a scientific way, and that the churches were trying to answer perfectly sound human questions. Though the answers were not acceptable, the questions themselves were and are perfectly acceptable, and perfectly legitimate.

As a matter of fact, contemporary existential and humanistic psychologists would probably consider a person sick or abnormal in an existential way if he were *not* concerned with these "religious" questions.

❧ III ❧

THE "CORE-RELIGIOUS," OR
"TRANSCENDENT," EXPERIENCE

The very beginning, the intrinsic core, the essence, the universal nucleus of every known high religion (unless Confucianism is also called a religion) has been the private, lonely, personal illumination, revelation, or ecstasy of some acutely sensitive prophet or seer. The high religions call themselves revealed religions and each of them tends to rest its validity, its function, and its right to exist on the codification and the communication of this original mystic experience or revelation from the lonely prophet to the mass of human beings in general.

But it has recently begun to appear that these "revelations" or mystical illuminations can be subsumed under the head of the "peak-experiences"[1] or "ecstasies" or

[1] If we were to go further with our analysis, we should find that, succeeding upon the discovery of the generality of all peak-experiences, there are also "specific" factors in each of the peak-experiences which differentiate them from each other to some extent. This relationship of specific to general is as figure to ground. It is something like that described by Spearman for "g" and "s" factors in intelligence

I do not discuss these "s" factors here because the "g" factor is far more important for the problem at hand and at this stage in its development.

"transcendent" experiences which are now being eagerly investigated by many psychologists. That is to say, it is very likely, indeed almost certain, that these older reports, phrased in terms of supernatural revelation, were, in fact, perfectly natural, human peak-experiences of the kind that can easily be examined today, which, however, were phrased in terms of whatever conceptual, cultural, and linguistic framework the particular seer had available in his time (Laski).

In a word, we can study today what happened in the past and was then explainable in supernatural terms only. By so doing, we are enabled to examine religion in all its facets and in all its meanings in a way that makes it a part of science rather than something outside and exclusive of it.

Also this kind of study leads us to another very plausible hypothesis: to the extent that all mystical or peak-experiences are the same in their essence and have always been the same, all religions are the same in their essence and always have been the same. They should, therefore, come to agree in principle on teaching that which is common to all of them, i.e., whatever it is that peak-experiences teach in common (whatever is *different* about these illuminations can fairly be taken to be localisms both in time and space, and are, therefore, peripheral, expendable, not essential). This something common, this something which is left over after we peel away all the localisms, all the accidents of particular languages or particular philosophies, all the ethnocentric phrasings, all those elements which are *not* common, we may call the "core-religious experience" or the "transcendent experience."

To understand this better, we must differentiate the prophets in general from the organizers or legalists in general as (abstracted) types. (I admit that the use of pure, extreme types which do not really exist can come close to the edge of caricature; nevertheless, I think it will help all of us in thinking through the problem we are here concerned with.) [2] The characteristic prophet is a lonely man who has discovered his truth about the world, the cosmos, ethics, God, and his own identity from within, from his own personal experiences, from what he would consider to be a revelation. Usually, perhaps always, the prophets of the high religions have had these experiences when they were alone.

Characteristically the abstraction-type of the legalist-ecclesiastic is the conserving organization man, an officer and arm of the organization, who is loyal to the structure of the organization which has been built up on the basis of the prophet's original revelation in order to make the revelation available to the masses. From everything we know about organizations, we may very well expect that people will become loyal to it, as well as to the original prophet and to his vision; or at least they will become loyal to the organization's version of the prophet's vision. I may go so far as to say that characteristically (and I mean not only the religious organizations but also parallel organizations like the Communist Party or like revolutionary groups) these organizations can be seen as a kind of punch card or IBM version of an original revelation or

[2] I have made no effort in this chapter, or in the next, to balance accounts by detailing the virtues and even the unavoidable necessity of organizations and organizers. I have written about these elsewhere (69).

mystical experience or peak-experience to make it suitable for group use and for administrative convenience.

It will be helpful here to talk about a pilot investigation, still in its beginnings, of the people I have called non-peakers. In my first investigations, in collaboration with Gene Nameche, I used this word because I thought some people had peak-experiences and others did not. But as I gathered information, and as I became more skillful in asking questions, I found that a higher and higher percentage of my subjects began to report peak-experiences. (See Appendix F on rhapsodic communication.) I finally fell into the habit of expecting everyone to have peak-experiences and of being rather surprised if I ran across somebody who could report none at all. Because of this experience, I finally began to use the word "non-peaker" to describe, not the person who is unable to have peak-experiences, but rather the person who is afraid of them, who suppresses them, who denies them, who turns away from them, or who "forgets" them. My preliminary investigations of the reasons for these negative reactions to peak-experiences have led me to some (unconfirmed) impressions about why certain kinds of people renounce their peak-experiences.

Any person whose character structure (or Weltanschauung, or way of life) forces him to try to be extremely or completely rational or "materialistic" or mechanistic tends to become a non-peaker. That is, such a view of life tends to make the person regard his peak- and transcendent experiences as a kind of insanity, a complete loss of control, a sense of being overwhelmed by irrational emotions, etc. The person who is afraid of going insane and who is, therefore, desperately hanging on to stability, control, reality, etc., seems to be frightened by peak-experiences and tends to fight them off. For the compulsive-obsessive person, who organizes his life around the denying and the controlling of emotion, the fear of being overwhelmed by an emotion (which is interpreted as a loss of control) is enough for him to mobilize all his stamping-out and defensive activities against the peak-experience. I have one instance of a very convinced Marxian who denied—that is, who turned away from—a legitimate peak-experience, finally classifying it as some kind of peculiar but unimportant thing that had happened but that had best be forgotten because this experience conflicted with her whole materialistic mechanistic philosophy of life. I have found a few non-peakers who were ultra-scientific, that is, who espoused the nineteenth-century conception of science as an unemotional or anti-emotional activity which was ruled entirely by logic and rationality and who thought anything which was not logical and rational had no respectable place in life. (I suspect also that extremely "practical," i.e., exclusively means-oriented, people will turn out to be non-peakers, since such experiences earn no money, bake no bread, and chop no wood. So also for extremely other-directed people, who scarcely know what is going on inside themselves. Perhaps also people who are reduced to the concrete à la Goldstein, etc. etc.) Finally, I should add that, in some cases, I could not come to any explanation for non-peaking.

If you will permit me to use this developing but not yet

validated vocabulary, I may then say simply that the relationship between the prophet and the ecclesiastic, between the lonely mystic and the (perfectly extreme)
religious-organization man may often be a relationship
between peaker and non-peaker. Much theology, much
verbal religion through history and throughout the world,
can be considered to be the more or less vain efforts
to put into communicable words and formulae, and into
symbolic rituals and ceremonies, the original mystical
experience of the original prophets. In a word, organized
religion can be thought of as an effort to communicate
peak-experiences to non-peakers, to teach them, to apply
them, etc. Often, to make it more difficult, this job falls
into the hands of non-peakers. On the whole we now would
expect that this would be a vain effort, at least so far as
much of mankind is concerned. The peak-experiences and
their experiential reality ordinarily are not transmittable
to non-peakers, at least not by words alone, and certainly
not by non-peakers. What happens to many people, especially the ignorant, the uneducated, the naïve, is that they
simply concretize all of the symbols, all of the words, all
of the statues, all of the ceremonies, and by a process of
functional autonomy make *them,* rather than the original
revelation, into the sacred things and sacred activities. That
is to say, this is simply a form of the idolatry (or fetish-
ism) which has been the curse of every large religion. In
idolatry the essential original meaning gets so lost in
concretizations that these finally become hostile to the
original mystical experiences, to mystics, and to prophets in
general, that is, to the very people that we might call from

our present point of view the truly religious people. Most religions have wound up denying and being antagonistic to the very ground upon which they were originally based.

If you look closely at the internal history of most of the world religions, you will find that each one very soon tends to divide into a left-wing and a right-wing, that is, into the peakers, the mystics, the transcenders, or the privately religious people, on the one hand, and, on the other, into those who concretize the religious symbols and metaphors, who worship little pieces of wood rather than what the objects stand for, those who take verbal formulas literally, forgetting the original meaning of these words, and, perhaps most important, those who take the organization, the church, as primary and as more important than the prophet and his original revelations. These men, like many organization men who tend to rise to the top in any complex bureaucracy, tend to be non-peakers rather than peakers. Dostoevski's famous Grand Inquisitor passage, in his *Brothers Karamazov*, says this in a classical way.

This cleavage between the mystics and the legalists, if I may call them that, remains at best a kind of mutual tolerance, but it has happened in some churches that the rulers of the organization actually made a heresy out of the mystic experiences and persecuted the mystics themselves. This may be an old story in the history of religion, but I must point out that it is also an old story in other fields. For instance, we can certainly say today that professional philosophers tend to divide themselves into the same kind of characterologically based left-wing and right-wing. Most official, orthodox philosophers today are the equivalent of

25

legalists who reject the problems and the data of transcendence as "meaningless." That is, they are positivists, atomists, analysts, concerned with means rather than with ends. They sharpen tools rather than discover truths. These people contrast sharply with another group of contemporary philosophers, the existentialists and the phenomenologists. These are the people who tend to fall back on experiencing as the primary datum from which everything starts.

A similar split can be detected in psychology, in anthropology, and, I am quite sure, in other fields as well, perhaps in *all* human enterprises. I often suspect that we are dealing here with a profoundly characterological or constitutional difference in people which may persist far into the future, a human difference which may be universal and may continue to be so. The job then will be to get these two kinds of people to understand each other, to get along well with each other, even to love each other. This problem is paralleled by the relations between men and women who are so different from each other and yet who *have to* live with each other and even to love each other. (I must admit that it would be almost impossible to achieve this with poets and literary critics, composers and music critics, etc.)

To summarize, it looks quite probable that the peak-experience may be the model of the religious revelation or the religious illumination or conversion which has played so great a role in the history of religions. But, because peak-experiences are in the natural world and because we

26

can research with them and investigate them, and because our knowledge of such experiences is growing and may be confidently expected to grow in the future, we may now fairly hope to understand more about the big revelations, conversions, and illuminations upon which the high religions were founded.

(Not only this, but I may add a new possibility for scientific investigation of transcendence. In the last few years it has become quite clear that certain drugs called "psychedelic," especially LSD and psilocybin, give us some possibility of control in this realm of peak-experiences. It looks as if these drugs often produce peak-experiences in the right people under the right circumstances, so that perhaps we needn't wait for them to occur by good fortune. Perhaps we can actually produce a private personal peak-experience under observation and whenever we wish under religious or non-religious circumstances. We may then be able to study in its moment of birth the experience of illumination or revelation. Even more important, it may be that these drugs, and perhaps also hypnosis, could be used to produce a peak-experience, with core-religious revelation, in non-peakers, thus bridging the chasm between these two separated halves of mankind.)

To approach this whole discussion from another angle, in effect what I have been saying is that the evidence from the peak-experiences permits us to talk about the essential, the intrinsic, the basic, the most fundamental religious or transcendent experience as a totally private and personal one which can hardly be shared (except with other "peak-ers"). As a consequence, all the paraphernalia of organized religion—buildings and specialized personnel, rituals, dogmas, ceremonials, and the like—are to the "peaker" secondary, peripheral, and of doubtful value in relation to the intrinsic and essential religious or transcendent experience. Perhaps they may even be very harmful in various ways. From the point of view of the peak-experiencer, each person has his own private religion, which he develops out of his own private revelations in which are revealed to him his own private myths and symbols, rituals and ceremonials, which may be of the profoundest meaning to him personally and yet completely idiosyncratic, i.e., of no meaning to anyone else. But to say it even more simply, each "peaker" discovers, develops, and retains his own religion (87).

In addition, what seems to be emerging from this new source of data is that this essential core-religious experience may be embedded either in a theistic, supernatural context or in a non-theistic context. This private religious experience is shared by all the great world religions including the atheistic ones like Buddhism, Taoism, Humanism, or Confucianism. As a matter of fact, I can go so far as to say that this intrinsic core-experience is a meeting ground not only, let us say, for Christians and Jews and Mohammedans but also for priests and atheists, for communists and anti-communists, for conservatives and liberals, for artists and scientists, for men and for women, and for different constitutional types, that is to say, for athletes and for poets, for thinkers and for doers. I say

28

this because our findings indicate that all or almost all people have or can have peak-experiences. Both men and women have peak-experiences, and all kinds of constitutional types have peak-experiences, but, although the content of the peak-experiences is approximately as I have described for all human beings (see Appendix A), the situation or the trigger which sets off peak-experience, for instance in males and females, can be quite different. These experiences can come from different sources, but their content may be considered to be very similar. To sum it up, from this point of view, the two religions of mankind tend to be the peakers and the non-peakers, that is to say, those who have private, personal, transcendent, core-religious experiences easily and often and who accept them and make use of them, and, on the other hand, those who have never had them or who repress or suppress them and who, therefore, cannot make use of them for their personal therapy, personal growth, or personal fulfillment.

❦ IV ❦

ORGANIZATIONAL DANGERS TO TRANSCENDENT EXPERIENCES

It has sometimes seemed to me as I interviewed "non-theistic religious people" that they had *more* religious (or transcendent) experiences than conventionally religious people. (This is, so far, only an impression but it would obviously be a worthwhile research project.) Partly this may have been because they were more often "serious" about values, ethics, life-philosophy, because they have had to struggle away from conventional beliefs and have had to create a system of faith for themselves individually. Various other determinants of this paradox also suggested themselves at various times, but I'll pass these by at this time.

The reason I now bring up this impression (which may or may not be validated, may or may not be simply a sampling error, etc.) is that it brought me to the realization that for most people a conventional religion, while strongly religionizing one part of life, thereby also strongly "de-religionizes" the rest of life. The experiences of the holy, the sacred, the divine, of awe, of creatureliness, of surrender, of mystery, of piety, thanksgiving, gratitude, self-dedication, if they happen at all, tend to be confined to a single day of the week, to happen under one roof only of one kind of structure only, under certain triggering circumstances only, to rest heavily on the presence of certain traditional, powerful, but intrinsically irrelevant, stimuli, e.g. organ music, incense, chanting of a particular kind, certain regalia, and other arbitrary triggers. Being religious, or rather feeling religious, under these ecclesiastical auspices seems to absolve many (most?) people from the necessity or desire to feel these experiences at any other time. "Religionizing" only one part of life secularizes the rest of it.

This is in contrast with my impression that "serious" people of all kinds tend to be able to "religionize" *any* part of life, *any* day of the week, in *any* place, and under all sorts of circumstances, i.e., to be aware of Tillich's "dimension of depth." Of course, it would not occur to the more "serious" people who are non-theists to put the label "religious experiences" on what they were feeling, or to use such words as "holy," "pious," "sacred," or the like. By my usage, however, they are often having "core-religious experiences" or transcendent experiences when they report having peak-experiences. In this sense, a sensitive, creative working artist I know who calls himself an agnostic could be said to be having many "religious experiences," and I am sure that he would agree with me if I asked him about it.

In any case, once this paradox is thought through, it ceases to be a paradox and becomes, instead, quite obvious.

If "heaven" is always available, ready to step into (70), and if the "unitive consciousness" (with its B-cognition, its perception of the realm of Being and the sacred and eternal) is always a possibility for any serious and thoughtful person, being to some extent under his own control (54), then having such "core-religious" or transcendental experiences is also to some extent under our own control, even apart from peak-experiences. (Having enough peak-experiences during which B-cognition takes place can lead to the probability of B-cognizing *without* peak-experiences.) I have also been able, by lecturing and by writing, to teach B-cognition and unitive consciousness, to some students at least. In principle, it is possible, through adequate understanding, to transform means-activities into end-activities, to "ontologize" (66); to see voluntarily under the aspect of eternity, to see the sacred and symbolic *in* and *through* the individual here-and-now instance.

What prevents this from happening? In general, all and any of the forces that diminish us, pathologize us, or that make us regress, e.g., ignorance, pain, illness, fear, "forgetting," dissociation, reduction to the concrete, neuroticizing, etc. That is, *not* having core-religious experiences may be a "lower," lesser state, a state in which we are not "fully functioning," not at our best, not fully human, not sufficiently integrated. When we are well and healthy and adequately fulfilling the concept "human being," then experiences of transcendence should in principle be commonplace.

Perhaps now what appeared to me first as a paradox can be seen as a matter of fact, not at all surprising. I had noticed something that had never before occurred to me, namely that orthodox religion can easily mean de-sacralizing much of life. It can lead to dichotomizing life into the transcendent and the secular-profane and can, therefore, compartmentalize and separate them temporally, spatially, conceptually, and experientially. This is in clear contradiction to the actualities of the peak-experiences. It even contradicts the traditionally religious versions of mystic experience, not to mention the experiences of satori, of Nirvana, and other Eastern versions of peak- and mystic experiences. All of these agree that the sacred and profane, the religious and secular, are not separated from each other. Apparently it is one danger of the legalistic and organizational versions of religion that they may tend to suppress naturalistic peak-, transcendent, mystical, or other core-religious experiences and to make them less likely to occur, i.e., the degree of religious organization may correlate negatively with the frequency of "religious" experiences.[1] Conventional religions may even be used as defenses against and resistances to the shaking experiences of transcendence.

There may also be another such inverse relationship—between organizationism and religious transcendent expe-

---

[1] I have just run across similar statements in Jung's autobiography (35). "The arch sin of faith, it seemed to me, was that it forestalled experience . . . and confirmed my conviction that in religious matters only experience counted" (p.92). "I am of course aware that theologians are in a more difficult situation than others. On the one hand they are closer to religion, but on the other hand they are more bound by church and dogma" (p. 94). (I hope that we are all aware that it is easier to be "pure" outside an organization, whether religious, political, economic, or, for that matter, scientific. And yet we cannot do without organizations. Perhaps one day we shall invent organizations that do not "freeze"?)

riencing—at least for some people. (For however many this may be, it is a *possible* danger for all.) If we contrast the vivid, poignant, shaking, peak-experience type of religious or transcendent experience, which I have been describing, with the thoughtless, habitual, reflex-like, absent-minded, automatic responses which are dubbed "religious" by many people (only because they occur in familiar circumstances semantically labelled "religious"), then we are faced with a universal, "existential" problem. Familiarization and repetition produces a lowering of the intensity and richness of consciousness, even though it *also* produces preference, security, comfort, etc. (55). Familiarization, in a word, makes it unnecessary to attend, to think, to feel, to live fully, to experience richly. This is true not only in the realm of religion but also in the realms of music, art, architecture, patriotism, even in nature itself.

If organized religion has any ultimate effects at all, it is through its power to shake the individual in his deepest insides. Words can be repeated mindlessly and without touching the intrapersonal depths, no matter how true or beautiful their meaning, so also for symbolic actions of any kind, e.g., saluting the flag, or for any ceremonies, rituals, or myths. They *can* be extremely important in their effects upon the person and, through him, upon the world. But this is true only if he experiences them, truly lives them. Only then do they have meaning and effect.

This is probably another reason why transcendent experiences seem to occur more frequently in people who have rejected their inherited religion and who have then created one for themselves (whether they call it that or not). Or, to be more cautious, this is what seems to occur in my sample, i.e., mostly college people. It is a problem not only for conservative religious organizations but also for liberal religious organizations, indeed for any organization of *any* kind.

And it will be just as true for educators when they will finally be forced to try to teach spirituality and transcendence. Education for patriotism in this country has been terribly disappointing to most profoundly patriotic Americans, so much so that just *these* people are apt to be called un-American. Rituals, ceremonies, words, formulae may touch some, but they do not touch many unless their meanings have been deeply understood and experienced. Clearly the aim of education in this realm must be phrased in terms of inner, subjective experiences in each individual. Unless these experiences are known to have occurred, value-education cannot be said to have succeeded in reaching its true goal.[2]

[2] The whole of Chapter I. "Religion Versus the Religious," (and especially the last two paragraphs) in John Dewey's *A Common Faith* are relevant to the theme of this chapter. As a matter of fact, the whole of Dewey's book should be read by anyone interested in my theses.

V

HOPE, SKEPTICISM, AND MAN'S HIGHER NATURE

The point of view that is rapidly developing now—that the highest spiritual values appear to have naturalistic sanctions and that supernatural sanctions for these values are, therefore, not necessary—raises some questions which have not been raised before in quite this form. For instance, why were supernatural sanctions for goodness, altruism, virtue, and love necessary in the first place?

Of course the question of the origins of religions as sanctions for ethics is terribly complex, and I certainly don't intend to be casual about it here. However, I can contribute one additional point which we can see more clearly today than ever before, namely that one important characteristic of the new "third" psychology is its demonstration of man's "higher nature." As we look back through the religious conceptions of human nature—and indeed we need not look back so very far because the same doctrine can be found in Freud—it becomes crystal clear that any doctrine of the innate depravity of man or any maligning of his animal nature very easily leads to some extra-human interpretation of goodness, saintliness, virtue, self-sacrifice, altruism, etc. If they can't be explained from within human nature—and explained they must be—then they must be explained from outside of human nature. The worse man is, the poorer a thing he is conceived to be, the more necessary becomes a god. It can also be understood more clearly now that one source of the decay of belief in supernatural sanctions has been increasing faith in the higher possibilities of human nature (on the basis of new knowledge).[1] Explanation from the natural is more parsimonious and therefore more satisfying to educated people than is explanation from the supernatural. The latter is therefore apt to be an inverse function of the former.

This process, however, has its costs; especially, I would guess, for the less sophisticated portions of the population, or at any rate for the more orthodoxly religious. For them, as Dostoievsky, Nietzsche, and others realized very clearly, "If God is dead, then anything is permitted, anything is possible." If the only sanction for "spiritual" values is supernatural, then undermining this sanction undermines *all* higher values.

Especially has this been true in recent decades, as positivistic science—which is for many the only theory of science—proved also to be an inadequate source of ethics and values. Faith in the rationalist millenium has also

---

[1] For instance, my studies of "self-actualizing people," i.e., fully evolved and developed people, make it clear that human beings at their best are far more admirable (godlike, heroic, great, divine, awe-inspiring, lovable, etc.) than ever before conceived, in their *own* proper nature. There is no need to add a non-natural determinant to account for saintliness, heroism, altruism, transcendence, creativeness; etc. Throughout history, human nature has been sold short primarily because of the lack of knowledge of the higher possibilities of man, of how far he can develop when permitted to.

been destroyed. The faith that ethical progress was an inevitable by-product of advances in knowledge of the natural world and in the technological by-products of these advances died with World War I, with Freud, with the depression, with the atom bomb. Perhaps even more shaking, certainly for the psychologist, has been the recent (61) discovery that affluence itself throws into the clearest, coldest light the spiritual, ethical, philosophical hunger of mankind. (This is so because striving for something one lacks inevitably makes one feel that life has a meaning and that life is worthwhile. But when one lacks nothing, and has nothing to strive for, then . . .?)

Thus we have the peculiar situation in which many intellectuals today find themselves skeptical in every sense, but fully aware of the yearning for a faith or a belief of some kind and aware also of the terrible spiritual (and political) consequences when this yearning has no satisfaction.[2]

And so we have a new language to describe the situation, words like anomie, anhedonia, rootlessness, value pathology, meaninglessness, existential boredom, spiritual starvation, other-directedness, the neuroses of success, etc. (See Appendix E.)

Most psychotherapists would agree that a large proportion of the population of all affluent nations—not only America—are now caught in this situation of valuelessness, although most of these therapists are still speaking superficially and symptomatically of character neuroses, immaturity, juvenile delinquency, over-indulgence, etc.

[2] See the February, 1950, issue of the *Partisan Review on* "Religion and the Intellectuals." See also Franklin L. Baumer, *Religion and the Rise of Skepticism* (New York: Harcourt, Brace & Co., 1960).

A new approach to psychotherapy, existential therapy, is evolving to meet this situation. But on the whole, since therapy is impracticable for mass purposes, most people simply stay caught in the situation and lead privately and publicly miserable lives. A small proportion "returns to traditional religion," although most observers agree that this return is not apt to be deeply rooted.

But some others, still a small proportion, are finding in newly available hints from psychology another possibility of a positive, naturalistic faith, a "common faith" as John Dewey called it, a "humanistic faith" as Erich Fromm called it, humanistic psychology as many others are now calling it. (See Appendix B.) As John MacMurray said, "Now is the point in history at which it becomes possible for man to adopt consciously as his own purpose the purpose which is already inherent in his own nature."—Quoted in *Man and God*, ed. V. Gollancz (Boston: Houghton Mifflin Co., 1951), p. 49. There is even a weekly journal, *Manas*, which could be said to be an organ for this new kind of faith and this new psychology.

VI

SCIENCE AND THE RELIGIOUS LIBERALS
AND NON-THEISTS

Nineteenth-century objectivistic, value-free science has finally proven to be also a poor foundation for the atheists, the agnostics, the rationalists, the humanists, and other non-theists, as well as for the "liberal" religionists, e.g., the Unitarians and the Universalists. Both of them, orthodox science and liberal and non-theistic religion, leave out too much that is precious to most human beings. In their revolt against the organized, institutionalized churches, they have unwittingly accepted the immature and naïve dichotomy between traditional religion (as the only carrier of values), on one hand, and, on the other, a totally mechanistic, reductionistic, objectivistic, neutral, value-free science. To this day, liberal religionists rest heavily, even exclusively, on the natural sciences which seem to them to be somehow more "scientific" than the psychological sciences upon which they should base themselves but which they use almost not at all (except in positivistic versions).

Thus, average, liberal religionists try to rest all their efforts on knowledge of the impersonal world rather than on the personal sciences. They stress rational knowledge and are uneasy with the irrational, the anti-rational, the non-rational, as if Freud and Jung and Adler had never lived. So they know nothing officially of a subrational unconscious, of repression, or of defensive processes in general, of resistances to insight, of impulses which are determinants of behavior and yet are unknown to the person himself. Like positivistic psychologists, they feel much more at home with the cognitive than they do with the emotional and the impulsive and volitional. They make no basic place in their systems for the mysterious, the unknown, the unknowable, the dangerous-to-know, or the ineffable. They pass by entirely the old, rich literature based on the mystical experiences. They have no systematic place for goals, ends, yearnings, aspirations, and hopes, let alone will or purpose. They don't know what to do with the experiential, the subjective, and the phenomenological that the existentialists stress so much, as do also the psychotherapists. The inexact, the illogical, the metaphorical, the mythic, the symbolic, the contradictory or conflicted, the ambiguous, the ambivalent are all considered to be "lower" or "not good," i.e., something to be "improved" toward pure rationality and logic. It is not yet understood that they are characteristic of the human being at his *highest* levels of development as well as at his lowest, and that they can be valued, used, loved, built upon, rather than just being swept under the rug. Nor is it sufficiently recognized that "good" as well as "bad" impulses can be repressed.

This is also true for the experiences of surrender, of

reverence, of devotion, of self-dedication, of humility and oblation, of awe and the feeling of smallness. These experiences, which organized religions have always tried to make possible, are also common enough in the peak-experiences and in the B-cognitions, including even impulses to kneeling, to prostration, and to something like worship. But these are all missing from the non-theisms and from the liberal theisms. This is of especial importance today because of the widespread "valuelessness" in our society, i.e., people have nothing to admire, to sacrifice themselves for, to surrender to, to die for.[1] This gap calls for filling. Perhaps, even, it may be an "instinctoid" need. Any onto-psychology or any religion, it would seem, must satisfy this need.

The result? A rather bleak, boring, unexciting, unemotional, cool philosophy of life which fails to do what the traditional religions have tried to do when they were at their best, to inspire, to awe, to comfort, to fulfill, to guide in the value choices, and to discriminate between higher and lower, better and worse, not to mention to produce Dionysiac experiences, wildness, rejoicing, impulsiveness.

[1] It should be noted (because it may contradict my thesis) that these general criticisms of the "liberal religions" apply also to the Quakers even though they originally based themselves in principle on inner, personal, quasi-mystic experience. Today, they, too, tend to be only Apollonian and have no respectable place for the Dionysian, for the "warm" as well as the "cool." They, too, are rational, "simple," sober, and decent, and bypass darkness, wildness, and craziness, hesitating, it appears, to stir up orgiastic emotions. They, too, have built themselves a philosophy of goodness that has no systematic place for evil. They have not yet incorporated Freud and Jung into their foundations, nor have they discovered that the depths of the personal unconscious are the source of joy, love, creativeness, play, and humor as well as of dangerous and crazy impulses.

Because I do not know enough about the Friends, I don't know why this is so. Certainly it is not because of any great reliance on nineteenth-century science.

Any religion, liberal or orthodox, theistic or non-theistic, must be not only intellectually credible and morally worthy of respect, but it must also be emotionally satisfying (and I include here the transcendent emotions as well).

No wonder that the liberal religions and semi-religious groups exert so little influence even though their members are the most intelligent and most capable sections of the population. It *must* be so just as long as they base themselves upon a lopsided picture of human nature which omits most of what human beings value, enjoy, and cherish in themselves, in fact, which they live for, and which they refuse to be done out of.

The theory of science which permits and encourages the exclusion of so much that is true and real and existent cannot be considered a comprehensive science. It is obviously not an organization of *everything* that is real. It doesn't integrate all the data. Instead of saying that these new data are "unscientific," I think we are now ready to turn the tables and change the definition of science so that it is able to include these data. (See Appendixes D and I.)

Some perceptive liberals and non-theists are going through an "agonizing reappraisal" very similar to that which the orthodox often go through, namely a loss of faith in their foundation beliefs. Just as many intellectuals lose faith in religious orthodoxy, so do they also lose faith in positivistic, nineteenth-century science as a way of life. Thus they too often have the sense of loss, the craving to believe, the yearning for a value-system, the valuelessness and the simultaneous longing for values which marks so many in this "Age of Longing" (6). (See also Appendix

43

E.) I believe that this need can be satisfied by a larger, more inclusive science, one which includes the data of transcendence.[2]

Not only must the liberal religions and the non-theisms accept and build upon all of these neglected aspects of human nature if they have any hope at all of fulfilling perfectly legitimate human needs, but also if these value-systems are to do the ultimate job of any social institution, i.e., to foster the fullest actualization and fulfillment of the highest and fullest humanness, then they will have to venture into even stranger fields of thought. For instance, such purely "religious" concepts as the sacred, the eternal, heaven and hell, the good death, and who knows what else as well are now being nibbled at by the encroaching naturalistic investigators. It looks as if these, too, will be brought into the human world. In any case, enough knowledge is already available so that I feel I can say very confidently that these concepts are *not* mere hallucinations, illusions, or delusions, or rather, more accurately, that they need not be. They can and do have referents in the real world.

I am myself uneasy, even jittery, over the semantic

[2] It was said of one man that "he could be at home neither with the Catholic solution of the religious problem nor with the rationalist dissolution of the problem." The "liberals" who gave up the illusion of a god modelled on a human father, who revolted against a wish-fulfillment god, against a churchly establishment with political ambitions and power, against functionally autonomous dogmas and rituals, also gave up, quite unnecessarily, the true and deep and necessary purposes of all "serious" humanists and humanistic religions: overcoming the limitations of a self-limited ego, relating in harmony to the cosmos, attempting to become all that a human being can, etc. (To the thoughtful scholar, interested in precursive answers to the same questions, I recommend an examination of New England transcendentalism and its interrelations with Unitarianism.)

confusion which lies in store for us—indeed which is already here—as all the concepts which have been traditionally "religious" are redefined and then used in a very different way. Even the word "god" is being defined by many theologians today in such a way as to exclude the conception of a person with a form, a voice, a beard, etc. If God gets to be defined as "Being itself," or as "the integrating principle in the universe," or as "the whole of everything," or as "the meaningfulness of the cosmos," or in some other non-personal way, then what will atheists be fighting against? They may very well agree with "integrating principles" or "the principle of harmony."

And if, as actually happened on one platform, Paul Tillich defined religion as "concern with ultimate concerns" and I then defined humanistic psychology in the same way, then what is the difference between a supernaturalist and a humanist?

The big lesson that must be learned here, not only by the non-theists and liberal religionists, but also by the supernaturalists, and by the scientists and the humanists, is that mystery, ambiguity, illogic, contradiction, mystic and transcendent experiences may now be considered to lie well within the realm of nature. These phenomena need not drive us to postulate additional supernatural variables and determinants. Even the unexplained and the presently unexplainable, ESP for instance, need not. And it is no longer accurate to accept them only as morbidities. The study of self-actualizing people has taught us differently (59, 67).

The other side of the coin needs examination, too. One

of the most irritating aspects of positivistic science is its overconfidence, I might call it, or perhaps its lack of humility. The pure, nineteenth-century scientist looks like a babbling child to sophisticated people just because he is so cocky, so self-assured, just because he doesn't know how little he knows, how limited scientific knowledge is when compared with the vast unknown.

Most powerfully is this true of the psychologist whose ratio of knowledge to mystery must be the smallest of all scientists. Indeed, sometimes I am so impressed by all that we need to know in comparison with what we do know that I think it best to define a psychologist, not as one who knows the answers, but rather as one who struggles with the questions.

Perhaps it is because he is so innocently unaware of his smallness, of the feebleness of his knowledge, of the smallness of his playpen, or the smallness of his portion of the cosmos and because he takes his narrow limits so for granted that he reminds me of the little boy who was seen standing uncertainly at a street corner with a bundle under his arm. A concerned bypasser asked him where he was going and he replied that he was running away from home. Why was he waiting at the corner? He wasn't allowed to cross the street!

Another consequence of accepting the concept of a natural, general, basic, personal religious experience is that it will also reform atheism, agnosticism, and humanism. These doctrines have, on the whole, been simply a rejection of the churches; and they have fallen into the trap of identifying religion with the churches, a very serious mistake as we have seen. They threw out too much, as we are now discovering. The alternative that these groups have rested on has been pure science of the nineteenth-century sort, pure rationalism insofar as they have not relied merely on negative attacks upon the organized churches. This has turned out to be not so much a solution of the problem as a retreat from it. But if it can be demonstrated that the religious questions (which were thrown out along with the churches) are valid questions, that these questions are almost the same as the deep, profound, and serious ultimate concerns of the sort that Tillich talks about and of the sort by which I would define humanistic psychology, then these humanistic sects could become much more useful to mankind than they are now.

As a matter of fact, they might very well become very similar to the reformed church organizations. It's quite possible that there wouldn't be much difference between them in the long run, if both groups accepted the primary importance and reality of the basic personal revelations (and their consequences) and if they could agree in regarding everything else as secondary, peripheral, and not necessary, not essentially defining characteristics of religion, they then could focus upon the examination of the personal revelations—the mystic experience, the peak-experience, the personal illumination—and of the B-cognitions which then ensue.

VII

VALUE-FREE EDUCATION?

These dichotomizing trends—making organized religions the guardian of all values, dichotomizing knowledge from religion, considering science to be value-free, and trying to make it so—have wrought their confusion in the field of education, too. The most charitable thing we can say about this state of affairs is that American education is conflicted and confused about its far goals and purposes. But for many educators, it must be said more harshly that they seem to have renounced far goals altogether or, at any rate, keep trying to. It is as if they wanted education to be purely technological training for the acquisition of skills which come close to being value-free or amoral (in the sense of being useful either for good or evil, and also in the sense of failing to enlarge the personality).

There are also many educators who *seem* to disagree with this technological emphasis, who stress the acquisition of pure knowledge, and who feel this to be the core of pure liberal education and the opposite of technological training. But it looks to me as if many of these educators are also value-confused, and it seems to me that they must remain so as long as they are not clear about the ultimate value of the acquisition of pure knowledge. Too often, it seems to me, pure knowledge has been given a kind of functionally autonomous, per se value, as was the case with Latin and Greek for young gentlemen and French and embroidery for young ladies. Why was this so? It was so because it *was* so, in the same way that someone recently defined a celebrity as one who is known for being known. These requirements may have had some functional validation long ago in their beginnings, but these reasons have long since been outgrown. This is an example of "functional autonomy" in Allport's sense: Knowledge has become independent of its origins, its motivations, its functions. It has become familiar and therefore self-validating. It tends to persist in spite of being non-functional or even anti-functional, in spite of frustrating (rather than satisfying) the needs which first gave it life.

Perhaps I can help to make my point clearer if I approach it from the other end, from the point of view of the ultimate goals of education. According to the new third psychology (See Appendix B), the far goal of education—as of psychotherapy, of family life, of work, of society, of life itself—is to aid the person to grow to fullest humanness, to the greatest fulfillment and actualization of his highest potentials, to his greatest possible stature. In a word, it should help him to become the best he is capable of becoming, to become *actually* what he deeply is *potentially*. What we call healthy growth is growth toward this final goal. And if this is the vectorial direction of education—the quarter of the compass toward which it moves, the purpose which gives it worth and meaning and which justifies it—then we are at once also supplied with a touchstone by which to discriminate good instruments from bad instruments, functional means from non-functional means, good teaching from bad teaching, good courses from bad courses, good curricula from bad curricula. The moment we can clearly distinguish instrumental goods from instrumental bads, thousands of consequences start to flow. (For the reasons that justify this as an empirical statement, see Appendix H.)

Another consequence of this new insight into the highest human end-goals and end-values is that it holds for every living human being. Furthermore, it holds from the moment of birth until the moment of death, even from before birth and after death in some very real senses. And, therefore, if education in a democracy is necessarily seen as helping every single person (not only an elite) toward his fullest humanness, then, in principle, education is properly a universal, ubiquitous, and life-long proposition. It implies education for all the human capacities, not only the cognitive ones. It implies education for feeble-minded people as well as intelligent ones. It implies education for adults as well as for children. And it implies that education is certainly not confined to the classroom.

And now I think the point must be clear that no subject matter is a sacred and eternal part of any fixed-for-all-time curriculum, e.g., of liberal arts. Any of the subjects we teach can be wrong for someone. Trying to teach algebra to a moron is idiotic, so is music for the tone-deaf, and painting for the color-blind, and, perhaps, even the details of the impersonal sciences for the person-centered kind of person. Such efforts don't fit the particular person and, therefore, must be at least partially a waste of time.

Many other kinds of educational foolishness are unavoidable by-products of current philosophical and axiological confusion in education. Trying to be value-free, trying to be purely technological (means without ends), trying to rest on tradition or habit alone (old values in the absence of living values), defining education simply as indoctrination (loyalty to ordained values rather than to one's own)—all these are value-confusions, philosophical and axiological failures. And inevitably, they breed all the value-pathologies, e.g., such idiocies as the four-year college degree,[1] three-credit courses,[2] required courses from which there is no exception, etc.[3] Clarity of end-values makes it very easy to avoid these mismatchings of means and ends. The better we know which ends we want, the easier it is for us to create truly efficient means to those ends. If we are *not* clear about those ends, or deny that there are any, then we are doomed to confusion of instru-

[1] "Isn't it a pity that my daughter left school in her senior year just before she finished her education?"

[2] Professor Pangloss would have been delighted by the fact that all human knowledge happens to fall apart into exactly the same three-credit slices, like the segments of a tangerine, and that they all happen to last for exactly the same number of class hours.

[3] "No man can call himself educated who doesn't know the *Iliad* (or constitutional law, or chemistry, or descriptive geometry, etc. etc.)." For that matter, one college I went to refused to give a degree unless the student could swim. Another one required that I take freshman composition even though I had articles in press for publication. Faculty politics are silly enough to supply us with many more examples than we need.

51

ments. We can't speak about efficiency unless we know efficiency for *what*. (I want to quote again that veritable symbol of our times, the test pilot who radioed back, "I'm lost, but I'm making record time.")

The final and unavoidable conclusion is that education—like all our social institutions—must be concerned with its final values, and this in turn is just about the same as speaking of what have been called "spiritual values" or "higher values." These are the principles of choice which help us to answer the age-old "spiritual" (philosophical? religious? humanistic? ethical?) questions: What is the good life? What is the good man? The good woman? What is the good society and what is my relation to it? What are my obligations to society? What is best for my children? What is justice? Truth? Virtue? What is my relation to nature, to death, to aging, to pain, to illness? How can I live a zestful, enjoyable, meaningful life? What is my responsibility to my brothers? Who *are* my brothers? What shall I be loyal to? What must I be ready to die for?

It used to be that all these questions were answered by organized religions in their various ways. Slowly these answers have come more and more to be based on natural, empirical fact and less and less on custom, tradition, "revelations," sacred texts, interpretations by a priestly class. What I have been pointing out in this lecture is that this process of a steadily increasing reliance on natural facts as guides in making life decisions is now advancing into the realm of "spiritual values." Partly this is so because of new discoveries, but partly it is so because more and more of us realize that nineteenth-century science has to be

52

redefined, reconstructed, enlarged, in order to be adequate to this new task. This job of reconstruction is now proceeding.

And insofar as education bases itself upon natural and scientific knowledge, rather than upon tradition, custom, the unexamined beliefs and prejudices of the community and of the conventional religious establishment, to that extent can I foresee that it, too, will change, moving steadily toward these ultimate values in its jurisdiction.

❧ VIII ❧

CONCLUSIONS

There is, then, a road which all profoundly "serious," "ultimately concerned" people of good will can travel together for a very long distance. Only when they come almost to its end does the road fork so that they must part in disagreement. Practically everything that, for example, Rudolf Otto (78) defines as characteristic of the religious experience—the holy; the sacred; creature feeling; humility; gratitude and oblation; thanksgiving; awe before the *mysterium tremendum;* the sense of the divine, the ineffable; the sense of littleness before mystery; the quality of exaltedness and sublimity; the awareness of limits and even of powerlessness; the impulse to surrender and to kneel; a sense of the eternal and of fusion with the whole of the universe; even the experience of heaven and hell— all of these experiences can be accepted as real by clergymen and atheists alike. And so it is also possible for all of them to accept in principle the empirical spirit and empirical methods and to humbly admit that knowledge is not complete, that it must grow, that it is in time and space, in history and in culture, and that, though it is relative to

54

man's powers and to his limits, it can yet come closer and closer to "The Truth" that is not dependent on man.

This road can be traveled together by all who are not afraid of truth, not only by theists and non-theists, but also by individuals of every political and economic persuasion, Russians and Americans, for instance.

What remains of disagreement? Only, it seems, the concept of supernatural beings or of supernatural laws or forces; and I must confess my feeling that by the time this forking of the road has been reached, this difference doesn't seem to be of any great consequence except for the comfort of the individual himself. Even the social act of belonging to a church must be a private act, with no great social or political consequences, once religious pluralism has been accepted, once any religion is seen as a local structure, in local terms, of species-wide, core-religious, transcendent experience.

Not only this, but it is also increasingly developing that leading theologians, and sophisticated people in general, define their god, not as a person, but as a force, a principle, a gestalt-quality of the whole of Being, an integrating power that expresses the unity and therefore the meaningfulness of the cosmos, the "dimension of depth," etc. At the same time, scientists are increasingly giving up the notion of the cosmos as a kind of simple machine, like a clock, or as congeries of atoms that clash blindly, having no relation to each other except push and pull, or as something that is final and eternal as it is and that is not evolving or growing. (As a matter of fact, nineteenth-century theologians also saw the world in a similar way, as some inert set of mechanisms; only for them, there was a Someone to set it into motion.)

These two groups (sophisticated theologians and sophisticated scientists) seem to be coming closer and closer together in their conception of the universe as "organismic," as having *some* kind of unity and integration, as growing and evolving and having direction and, therefore, having *some* kind of "meaning." Whether or not to call this integration "God" finally gets to be an arbitrary decision and a personal indulgence determined by one's personal history, one's personal revelations, and one's personal myths. John Dewey, an agnostic, decided for strategic and communicative purposes to retain the word "God," defining it in a naturalistic way (14). Others have decided against using it also for strategic reasons. What we wind up with is a new situation in the history of the problem in which a "serious" Buddhist, let us say, one who is concerned with "ultimate concerns" and with Tillich's "dimension of depth," is more co-religionist to a "serious" agnostic than he is to a conventional, superficial, other-directed Buddhist for whom religion is only habit or custom, i.e., "behavior."

Indeed, these "serious" people are coming so close together as to suggest that they are becoming a single party of mankind, the earnest ones, the seeking, questioning, probing ones, the ones who are not sure, the ones with a "tragic sense of life," the explorers of the depths and of the heights, the "saving remnant." The other party then is made up of all the superficial, the moment-bound, the here-bound ones, those who are totally absorbed with the trivial, those who are "plated with piety, not alloyed with it," those who are reduced to the concrete, to the momentary, and to the immediately selfish.[1] Almost, we could say, we wind up with adults, on the one hand, and children, on the other.

What is the practical upshot for education of all these considerations? We wind up with a rather startling conclusion, namely, that the teaching of spiritual values of ethical and moral values definitely does (in principle) have a place in education, perhaps ultimately a very basic and essential place, and that this in no way needs to controvert the American separation between church and state for the very simple reason that spiritual, ethical, and moral values need have nothing to do with any church. Or perhaps, better said, they are the common core of all churches, all religions, including the non-theistic ones. As a matter of fact, it is possible that precisely these ultimate values are and should be the far goals of all education, as they are and should be also the far goals of psychotherapy, of child care, of marriage, the family, of work, and perhaps of all other social institutions. I grant that this may turn out to be an overstatement, and yet there is something here that we must all accept. We reject the notion of distant value-goals in education under the penalty of falling into the great danger of defining education as mere technological training without relation to the good life, to ethics, to morals, or for that matter to anything else. Any philosophy that permits facts to become amoral, totally separated from values, makes possible in theory at least the Nazi

[1] Baumer (6) speaks of such people who can "be recognized precisely by the fact that the fundamental questions are no longer mentioned at all by these true secularists" (p. 234).

physician "experimenting" in the concentration camps, or the spectacle of captured German engineers working devotedly for whichever side happened to capture them.

Education must be seen as at least partially an effort to produce the good human being, to foster the good life and the good society. Renouncing this is like renouncing the reality and the desirability of morals and ethics. Furthermore, "An education which leaves untouched the entire region of transcendental thought is an education which has nothing important to say about the meaning of human life."—*Manas* (July 17, 1963).

RELIGIOUS ASPECTS OF PEAK-EXPERIENCES

Practically everything that happens in the peak-experiences, naturalistic though they are, could be listed under the headings of religious happenings, or indeed have been in the past considered to be only religious experiences.

1. For instance, it is quite characteristic in peak-experiences that the whole universe is perceived as an integrated and unified whole. This is not as simple a happening as one might imagine from the bare words themselves. To have a clear perception (rather than a purely abstract and verbal philosophical acceptance) that the universe is all of a piece and that one has his place in it—one is a part of it, one belongs in it—can be so profound and shaking an experience that it can change the person's character and his Weltanschauung forever after. In my own experience I have two subjects who, because of such an experience, were totally, immediately, and permanently cured of (in one case) chronic anxiety neurosis and (in the other case) of strong obsessional thoughts of suicide.

This, of course, is a basic meaning of religious faith for many people. People who might otherwise lose their "faith" will hang onto it because it gives a meaningfulness to the universe, a unity, a single philosophical explanation which makes it all hang together. Many orthodoxly religious people would be so frightened by giving up the notion that the universe has integration, unity, and, therefore, meaningfulness (which is given to it by the fact that it was all created by God or ruled by God or *is* God) that the only alternative for them would be to see the universe as a totally unintegrated chaos.

2. In the cognition that comes in peak-experiences, characteristically the percept is exclusively and fully attended to. That is, there is tremendous concentration of a kind which does not normally occur. There is the truest and most total kind of visual perceiving or listening or feeling. Part of what this involves is a peculiar change which can best be described as non-evaluating, non-comparing, or non-judging cognition. That is to say, figure and ground are less sharply differentiated. Important and unimportant are also less sharply differentiated, i.e., there is a tendency for things to become equally important rather than to be ranged in a hierarchy from very important to quite unimportant. For instance, the mother examining in loving ecstasy her new-born infant may be enthralled by every single part of him, one part as much as another one, one little toenail as much as another little toenail, and be struck into a kind of religious awe in this way. This same kind of total, non-comparing acceptance of everything, as if everything were equally important, holds also for the perception of people. Thus it comes about that in peak-

experience cognition a person is most easily seen per se, in himself, by himself, uniquely and idiosyncratically as if he were the sole member of his class. Of course, this is a very common aspect not only of religious experience but of most theologies as well, i.e., the person is unique, the person is sacred, one person in principle is worth as much as any other person, everyone is a child of God, etc.

3. The cognition of being (B-cognition) that occurs in peak-experiences tends to perceive external objects, the world, and individual people as more detached from human concerns. Normally we perceive everything as relevant to human concerns and more particularly to our own private selfish concerns. In the peak-experiences, we become more detached, more objective, and are more able to perceive the world as if it were independent not only of the perceiver but even of human beings in general. The perceiver can more readily look upon nature as if it were there in itself and for itself, not simply as if it were a human playground put there for human purposes. He can more easily refrain from projecting human purposes upon it. In a word, he can see it in its own Being (as an end in itself) rather than as something to be used or something to be afraid of or something to wish for or to be reacted to in some other personal, human, self-centered way. That is to say, B-cognition, because it makes human irrelevance more possible, enables us thereby to see more truly the nature of the object in itself. This is a little like talking about god-like perception, superhuman perception. The peak-experience seems to lift us to greater than normal

heights so that we can see and perceive in a higher than usual way. We become larger, greater, stronger, bigger, taller people and tend to perceive accordingly.

4. To say this in a different way, perception in the peak-experiences can be relatively ego-transcending, self-forgetful, egoless, unselfish. It can come closer to being unmotivated, impersonal, desireless, detached, not needing or wishing. Which is to say, that it becomes more object-centered than ego-centered. The perceptual experience can be more organized around the object itself as a centering point rather than being based upon the selfish ego. This means in turn that objects and people are more readily perceived as having independent reality of their own.

5. The peak-experience is felt as a self-validating, self-justifying moment which carries its own intrinsic value with it. It is felt to be a highly valuable—even uniquely valuable—experience, so great an experience sometimes that even to attempt to justify it takes away from its dignity and worth. As a matter of fact, so many people find this so great and high an experience that it justifies not only itself but even living itself. Peak-experiences can make life worthwhile by their occasional occurrence. They give meaning to life itself. They prove it to be worthwhile. To say this in a negative way, I would guess that peak-experiences help to prevent suicide.

6. Recognizing these experiences as end-experiences rather than as means-experiences makes another point. For one thing, it proves to the experiencer that there are ends in the world, that there are things or objects or expe-

riences to yearn for which are worthwhile in themselves. This in itself is a refutation of the proposition that life and living is meaningless. In other words, peak-experiences are one part of the operational definition of the statement that "life is worthwhile" or "life is meaningful."

7. In the peak-experience there is a very·characteristic disorientation in time and space, or even the lack of consciousness of time and space. Phrased positively, this is like experiencing universality and eternity. Certainly we have here, in a very operational sense, a real and scientific meaning of "under the aspect of eternity." This kind of timelessness and spacelessness contrasts very sharply with normal experience. The person in the peak-experiences may feel a day passing as if it were minutes or also a minute so intensely lived that it might feel like a day or a year or an eternity even. He may also lose his consciousness of being located in a particular place.

8. The world seen in the peak-experiences is seen only as beautiful, good, desirable, worthwhile, etc. and is never experienced as evil or undesirable. The world is accepted. People will say that then they understand it. Most important of all for comparison with religious thinking is that somehow they become reconciled to evil. Evil itself is accepted and understood and seen in its proper place in the whole, as belonging there, as unavoidable, as necessary, and, therefore, as proper. Of course, the way in which I (and Laski also) gathered peak-experiences was by asking for reports of ecstasies and raptures, of the most blissful and perfect moments of life. Then, of course, life

would look beautiful. And then all the foregoing might seem like discovering something that had been put in a priori. But observe that what I am talking about is the perception of evil, of pain, of disease, of death. In the peak-experiences, not only is the world seen as acceptable and beautiful, but, and this is what I am stressing, the bad things about life are accepted more totally than they are at other times. It is as if the peak-experience reconciled people to the presence of evil in the world.

9. Of course, this is another way of becoming "god-like." The gods who can contemplate and encompass the whole of being and who, therefore, understand it must see it as good, just, inevitable, and must see "evil" as a product of limited or selfish vision and understanding. If we could be god-like in this sense, then we, too, out of universal understanding would never blame or condemn or be disappointed or shocked. Our only possible emotions would be pity, charity, kindliness, perhaps sadness or amusement. But this is precisely the way in which self-actualizing people do at times react to the world, and in which all of us react in our peak-experiences.

10. Perhaps my most important finding was the discovery of what I am calling B-values or the intrinsic values of Being. (See Appendix G.) When I asked the question, "How does the world look different in peak-experiences?", the hundreds of answers that I got could be boiled down to a quintessential list of characteristics which, though they overlap very much with one another can still be considered as separate for the sake of research. What is important for us in this context is that this list of the described character-

64

istics of the world as it is perceived in our most perspicuous moments is about the same as what people through the ages have called eternal verities, or the spiritual values, or the highest values, or the religious values. What this says is that facts and values are not totally different from each other; under certain circumstances, they fuse. Most religions have either explicitly or by implication affirmed some relationship or even an overlapping or fusion between facts and values. For instance, people not only existed but they were also sacred. The world was not only merely existent but it was also sacred (54).

11. B-cognition in the peak-experience is much more passive and receptive, much more humble, than normal perception is. It is much more ready to listen and much more able to hear.

12. In the peak-experience, such emotions as wonder, awe, reverence, humility, surrender, and even worship before the greatness of the experience are often reported. This may go so far as to involve thoughts of death in a peculiar way. Peak-experiences can be so wonderful that they can parallel the experience of dying, that is of an eager and happy dying. It is a kind of reconciliation and acceptance of death. Scientists have never considered as a scientific problem the question of the "good death"; but here in these experiences we discover a parallel to what has been considered to be the religious attitude toward death, i.e., humility or dignity before it, willingness to accept it, possibly even a happiness with it.

13. In peak-experiences, the dichotomies, polarities, and conflicts of life tend to be transcended or resolved. That is

to say, there tends to be a moving toward the perception of unity and integration in the world. The person himself tends to move toward fusion, integration, and unity and away from splitting, conflicts, and oppositions.

14. In the peak-experiences, there tends to be a loss, even though transient, of fear, anxiety, inhibition, of defense and control, of perplexity, confusion, conflict, of delay and restraint. The profound fear of disintegration, of insanity, of death, all tend to disappear for the moment. Perhaps this amounts to saying that fear disappears.

15. Peak-experiences sometimes have immediate effects or aftereffects upon the person. Sometimes their aftereffects are so profound and so great as to remind us of the profound religious conversions which forever after changed the person. Lesser effects could be called therapeutic. These can range from very great to minimal or even to no effects at all. This is an easy concept for religious people to accept, accustomed as they are to thinking in terms of conversions, of great illuminations, of great moments of insight, etc.

16. I have likened the peak-experience in a metaphor to a visit to a personally defined heaven from which the person then returns to earth. This is like giving a naturalistic meaning to the concept of heaven. Of course, it is quite different from the conception of heaven as a place somewhere into which one physically steps after life on this earth is over. The conception of heaven that emerges from the peak-experiences is one which exists all the time all around us, always available to step into for a little while at least.

17. In peak-experiences, there is a **tendency to move** more closely to a perfect identity, or uniqueness, or to the idiosyncracy of the person or to his real self, to have become more a real person.

18. The person feels himself more than at other times to be responsible, active, the creative center of his own activities and of his own perceptions, more self-determined, more a free agent, with more "free will" than at other times.

19. But it has also been discovered that precisely those persons who have the clearest and strongest identity are exactly the ones who are most able to transcend the ego or the self and to become selfless, who are at least relatively selfless and relatively egoless.

20. The peak-experiencer becomes more loving and more accepting, and so he becomes more spontaneous and honest and innocent.

21. He becomes less an object, less a thing, less a thing of the world living under the laws of the physical world, and he becomes more a psyche, more a person, more subject to the psychological laws, especially the laws of what people have called the "higher life."

22. Because he becomes more unmotivated, that is to say, closer to non-striving, non-needing, non-wishing, he asks less for himself in such moments. He is less selfish. (We must remember that the gods have been considered generally to have no needs or wants, no deficiencies, no lacks, and to be gratified in all things. In this sense, the unmotivated human being becomes more god-like.)

23. People during and after peak-experiences charac-

teristically feel lucky, fortunate, graced. A common reaction is "I don't deserve this." A common consequence is a feeling of gratitude, in religious persons, to their God, in others, to fate or to nature or to just good fortune. It is interesting in the present context that this can go over into worship, giving thanks, adoring, giving praise, oblation, and other reactions which fit very easily into orthodox religious frameworks. In that context we are accustomed to this sort of thing—that is, to the feeling of gratitude or all-embracing love for everybody and for everything, leading to an impulse to do something good for the world, an eagerness to repay, even a sense of obligation and dedication.

24. The dichotomy or polarity between humility and pride tends to be resolved in the peak-experiences and also in self-actualizing persons. Such people resolve the dichotomy between pride and humility by fusing them into a single complex superordinate unity, that is by being proud (in a certain sense)and also humble (in a certain sense). Pride (fused with humility) is not hubris nor is it paranoia; humility (fused with pride) is not masochism.

25. What has been called the "unitive consciousness" is often given in peak-experiences, i.e., a sense of the sacred glimpsed *in* and *through* the particular instance of the momentary, the secular, the worldly.

❧ Appendix B ❧

THE THIRD PSYCHOLOGY

The following description of the "Third Psychology" is taken from the Preface of my book *Toward a Psychology of Being*.[1]

A word about contemporary intellectual currents in psychology may help to locate this book in its proper place. The two comprehensive theories of human nature most influencing psychology until recently have been the Freudian and the experimentalistic-positivistic-behavioristic. All other theories were less comprehensive and their adherents formed many splinter groups. In the last few years, however, these various groups have rapidly been coalecsing into a third, increasingly comprehensive theory of human nature, into what might be called a "Third Force." This group includes the Adlerians, Rankians, and Jungians, as well as the neo-Freudians (or neo-Adlerians) and the post-Freudians (psychoanalytic ego-psychologists as well as writers like Marcuse, Wheelis, Erikson, Marmor, Szasz, N. Brown, H. Lynd, and Schachtel, who are taking over from the Talmudic psychoanalysts). In addition, the influence of Kurt Goldstein and his organismic-psychology is steadily

[1] From Maslow's *Toward a Psychology of Being*, Copyright 1962, D. Van Nostrand Company, Inc., Princeton, N. J.

growing. So also is that of Gestalt therapy, of the Gestalt and Lewinian psychologists, of the general-semanticists, and of such personality-psychologists as G. Allport, G. Murphy, J. Moreno and H. A. Murray. A new and powerful influence is existential psychology and psychiatry. Dozens of other major contributors can be grouped as Self-psychologists, phenomenological psychologists, growth-psychologists, Rogerian psychologists, humanistic psychologists, and so on and so on and so on. A full list is impossible. A simpler way of grouping these is available in the five journals in which this group is most apt to publish, all relatively new. These are the *Journal of Individual Psychology* (University of Vermont, Burlington, Vt.), the *American Journal of Psychoanalysis* (220 W. 98th St., New York, N. Y.), the *Journal of Existential Psychiatry* (679 N. Michigan Ave., Chicago, Ill.), the *Review of Existential Psychology and Psychiatry* (Duquesne University, Pittsburgh, Pa.), and the newest one, the *Journal of Humanistic Psychology* (Station A, P.O. Box 11772, Palo Alto, Calif.). In addition, the journal *Manas* (P. O. Box 32,112, El Sereno Station, Los Angeles, Calif.) applies this point of view to the personal and social philosophy of the intelligent layman.

This brief statement of the purposes of the *Journal of Humanistic Psychology* was made by its editor, Anthony Sutich, and agreed to by its editorial board:

The *Journal of Humanistic Psychology* publishes papers dealing with Humanistic Psychology, defined as "primarily an orientation toward the whole of psychology rather than a distinct area or school. It stands for respect for the worth of persons, respect for differences of approach, open-mindedness as to acceptable methods, and interest in exploration of new aspects of human behavior. As a "third force" in contemporary psychology it is concerned with topics having

70

little place in existing theories and systems; e.g., love, creativity, self, growth, organism, basic need-gratification, self-actualization, higher values, being, becoming, spontaneity, play, humor, affection, naturalness, warmth, ego-transcendence, objectivity, autonomy, responsibility, meaning, fairplay, transcendental experience, peak experience, courage, and related concepts. (This approach finds expression in the writings of such persons as Allport, Angyal, Asch, Bühler, Fromm, Goldstein, Horney, Maslow, Moustakas, Rogers, Wertheimer, and in certain of the writings of Jung, Adler, and the psychoanalytic ego-psychologists, and existential and phenomenological psychologists).

For additional statements on the Third Psychology, see the Bibliography, entries 4, 9, 12, 13, 20, 24, 29, 34, 70, 75, 80, and 82.

❦ Appendix C ❦

ETHNOCENTRIC PHRASINGS OF PEAK-EXPERIENCES

It has been demonstrated again and again that the transcendent experiences have occurred to some people in any culture and at any time and of any religion and in any caste or class. All these experiences are described in about the same general way; the language and the concrete contents may be different, indeed must be different. These experiences are essentially ineffable (in the sense that even the best verbal phrasings are not quite good enough), which is also to say that they are unstructured (like Rorschach ink-blots). Also throughout history, they have never been understood in a naturalistic way. Small wonder it is then that the mystic, trying to describe his experience, can do it only in a local, culture-bound, ignorance-bound, language-bound way, confusing his description of the experience with whatever explanation of it and phrasing of it is most readily available to him in his time and in his place.

Laski (42) discusses the problem in detail in her chapters on "Overbeliefs" and in other places and agrees with

James in disregarding them. For instance, she points out (p. 14), "To a substantial extent the people in the religious group knew the vocabulary for such experiences before they knew the experience; inevitably when the experiences are known, they tend to be recounted in the vocabulary already accepted as appropriate."

Koestler (39) also said it well, "But because the experience is inarticulate, has no sensory shape, color or words, it lends itself to transcription in many forms, including visions of the cross, or of the goddess Kali; they are like dreams of a person born blind. . . . Thus a genuine mystic experience may mediate a *bona fide* conversion to practically any creed, Christianity, Buddhism or Fire-Worship" (p. 353). In the same volume, Koestler reports in vivid detail a mystic experience of his own.

Still another way of understanding this phenomenon is to liken the peak-experiences to raw materials which can be used for different *styles* of structures, as the same bricks and mortar and lumber would be built into different kinds of houses by a Frenchman, a Japanese, or a Tahitian (45).

I have, therefore, paid no attention to these localisms since they cancel one another out. I take the generalized peak-experience to be that which is common to all places and times.

Appendix D

WHAT IS THE VALIDITY OF KNOWLEDGE GAINED IN PEAK-EXPERIENCES?

This question is too huge and too important for a small space. All I can do here is to try to make a prima facie case for taking the question seriously. Both the question and the answers can be more clearly conceived and phrased today than ever before. This is so mostly because the mystic experience has been detached from local religious creeds and brought into the realm of nature and, therefore, of science. The questions can be more specific and, furthermore, can often be phrased in a confirmable-disconfirmable way.

In addition, it appears quite clear that the kind of (putative) knowledge gained in peak-experiences can also be obtained from desolation experiences. Furthermore, these insights may become independent of peak-experiences, and thereafter be available under more ordinary circumstances. (The way in which I have phrased this in my own vocabulary is: B-knowledge, B-cognition, and peak-experiences may occur independently of each other.) It is also possible that there is a kind of "serene," non-ecstatic B-cognition, but I am much less sure of this.

The question has to be differentiated still further. There is no doubt that great insights and revelations are profoundly felt in mystic or peak-experiences, and certainly some of these are, *ipso facto*, intrinsically valid *as experiences*. That is, one can and does learn from such experiences that, e.g., joy, ecstasy, and rapture do in fact exist and that they are in principle available for the experiencer, even if they never have been before. Thus the peaker learns surely and certainly that life *can* be worthwhile, that it *can* be beautiful and valuable. There *are* ends in life, i.e., experiences which are so precious in themselves as to prove that not everything is a means to some end other than itself.

Another kind of self-validating insight is the experience of being a real identity, a real self, of feeling what it is like to feel really oneself, what in fact one is—not a phony, a fake, a striver, an impersonator. Here again, the experiencing itself is the revelation of a truth.

My feeling is that if it were never to happen again, the power of the experience could permanently affect the attitude toward life. A single glimpse of heaven is enough to confirm its existence even if it is never experienced again. It is my strong suspicion that even one such experience might be able to prevent suicide, for instance, and perhaps many varieties of slow self-destruction, e.g., alcoholism, drug-addiction, addiction to violence, etc. I would guess also, on theoretical grounds, that peak-experiences might very well abort "existential meaninglessness," states of valuelessness, etc., at least occasionally. (These deductions from the nature of intense peak-experiences are given some support by general experience with LSD and psilocybin. Of course these preliminary reports also await confirmation.)

This then is one kind of peak-knowledge of whose validity and usefulness there can be no doubt, any more than there could be with discovering for the first time that the color "red" exists and is wonderful. Joy exists, can be experienced and feels very good indeed, and one can always hope that it will be experienced again.

Perhaps I should add here the paradoxical result—for some—that death may lose its dread aspect. Ecstasy is somehow close to death-experience, at least in the simple, empirical sense that death is often mentioned during reports of peaks, *sweet* death that is. After the acme, only less is possible. In any case, I have occasionally been told, "I felt that I could willingly die," or, "No one can ever again tell me death is bad," etc. Experiencing a kind of "sweet death" may remove its frightening aspect. This observation should, of course, be studied far more carefully than I have been able to. But the point is that the experience itself is a kind of knowledge gained (or attitude changed) which is self-validating. Other such experiences, coming for the first time, are true simply because experienced, e.g., greater integration of the organism, experiencing physiognomic perception, fusing primary- and secondary-process, fusing knowing and valuing, transcending dichotomies, experiencing knowing as being, etc., etc. The widening and enriching of consciousness through new perceptual experiences, many of which leave a lasting effect, is a little like improving the perceiver himself.

More frequently, however, peak-knowledge *does* need external, independent validation (70) or at least the request for such validation is a meaningful request; for instance, falling in love leads not only to greater care, which means closer attention, examination, and, therefore, greater knowledge, but it may also lead to affirmative statements and judgments which may be untrue however touching and affecting they may also be, e.g., "my husband is a genius."

The history of science and invention is full of instances of validated peak-insights and also of "insights" that failed. At any rate, there are enough of the former to support the proposition that the knowledge obtained in peak-insight-experiences *can* be validated and valuable.

This is also true sometimes for the awe-inspiring, poignant insights (both of peak type and also of the desolation type) or revelations that can come in psychotherapy—even though not very frequently. This falling of the veils can be a valid perception of what has not been consciously perceived before.

This all seems very obvious and very simple. Why has there then been such flat rejection of this path to knowledge? Partly I suppose the answer is that this kind of revelation–knowledge does not make four apples visible where there were only three before, nor do the apples change into bananas. No! it is more a shift in attention, in the organization of perception, in noticing or realizing, that occurs.

In peak-experiences, several kinds of attention-change

can lead to new knowledge. For one, love, fascination, absorption can frequently mean "looking intensely, with care," as already mentioned. For another, fascination can mean great intensity, narrowing and focussing of attention, and resistance to distraction of any kind, or of boredom or even fatigue. Finally, what Bucke (10) called Cosmic Consciousness involves an attention-widening so that the whole cosmos is perceived as a unity, and one's place in this whole is simultaneously perceived.

This new "knowledge" can be a change in attitude, valuing reality in a different way, seeing things from a new perspective, from a different centering point. Possibly a good many instances could come under the head of gestalt-perception, i.e., of seeing chaos in a newly organized way—or of shifting from one gestalt to another, of breaking up an imbeddedness or creating a new one, changing figure-ground relationships, of making a better gestalt, of closure, in a word, of the cognition of relationships and their organization.

Another kind of cognitive process which can occur in peak-experiences is the freshening of experience and the breaking up of rubricizing (59). Familiarization dulls cognition, especially in anxious people, and it is then possible to walk through all sorts of miraculous happenings without experiencing them as such. In peaks, the miraculous "suchness" of things can break through into consciousness. This is a basic function of art, and could be studied in that realm also. This kind of "innocent perception" is described in one of my articles (63). It is a kind of perspicuity which contrasts with what can only be called "normal blindness."

A subcategory of this renewed perception of what lies before our eyes is the peak-perception of the fact that truisms are true, e.g., it is wonderful to be understood, virtue is self-rewarding, sunsets are beautiful, money is not everything, etc. These "platitudes" can be rediscovered again and again in peak-moments. They, too, are examples of the new depth and penetration possible in such moments when life is seen freshly as if for the first time, and as if never seen before. So also is the experience of gratitude, of appreciation for good fortune, of grace.

In Appendix I and elsewhere in this essay, I have spoken of unitive perception, i.e., fusion of the B-realm with the D-realm, fusion of the eternal with the temporal, the sacred with the profane, etc. Someone has called this "the measureless gap between the poetic perception of reality and prosaic, unreal commonsense." Anyone who cannot perceive the sacred, the eternal, the symbolic, is simply blind to an aspect of reality, as I think I have amply demonstrated elsewhere (54), and in Appendix I.

For "ought perception," "ontification" and other examples of B-knowledge, see my article "Fusions of Facts and Values" (54). The bibliography of this paper refers to the literature of gestalt psychology for which I have no room here. For "reduction to the concrete" and its implications for cognition of abstractness in various senses, Goldstein (23, 24) should be consulted. Peak-experiencers often report something that might be called a particular kind of abstract perception, i.e., perception of essence, of "the hidden order of things, the X-ray texture of the world, normally obscured by layers of irrelevancy" (39, p. 352). My paper on isomorphism (48) also contains relevant data, of which I will mention here only the factor of being "worthy of the experience," of deserving it, or of being up to it. Health brings one "up to" higher levels of reality; peak-experiences can be considered a transient self-actualization of the person. It can therefore be understood as lifting him "higher," making him "taller," etc., so that he becomes "deserving" of more difficult truths, e.g., only integration can perceive integration, only the one who is capable of love can cognize love, etc.

Non-interfering, receptive, Taoistic perception is necessary for the perception of certain kinds of truth (49). Peak-experiences are states in which striving, interfering, and active controlling diminish, thereby permitting Taoistic perception, thereby diminishing the effect of the perceiver upon the percept. Therefore, truer knowledge (of some things) may be expected and has been reported.

To summarize, the major changes in the status of the problem of the validity of B-knowledge, or illumination-knowledge, are: (A) shifting it away from the question of the reality of angels, etc., i.e., naturalizing the question; (B) affirming experientially valid knowledge, the intrinsic validity of the enlarging of consciousness, i.e., of a wider range of experiencing; (C) realizing that the knowledge revealed was there all the time, ready to be perceived, if only the perceiver were "up to it," ready for it. This is a change in perspicuity, in the efficiency of the perceiver, in his spectacles, so to speak, *not* a change in the nature of reality or the invention of a new piece of reality which wasn't there before. The word "psychedelic" (consciousness-expanding) may be used here. Finally, (D) this kind of knowledge can be achieved in other ways; we need not rely solely on peak-experiences or peak-producing drugs for its attainment. There are more sober and laborious—and perhaps, therefore, better in some ways in the long run—avenues to achieving transcendent knowledge (B-knowledge). That is, I think we shall handle the problem better if we stress ontology and epistemology rather than the triggers and the stimuli.

❧ Appendix E ❧

PREFACE TO "NEW KNOWLEDGE IN HUMAN VALUES" [1]

This volume springs from the belief, first that the ultimate disease of our time is valuelessness; second, that this state is more crucially dangerous than ever before in history; and finally, that something can be done about it by man's own rational efforts.

The state of valuelessness has been variously described as anomie, amorality, anhedonia, rootlessness, emptiness, hopelessness, the lack of something to believe in and to be devoted to. It has come to its present dangerous point because all the traditional value systems ever offered to mankind have in effect proved to be failures (our present state proves this to be so). Furthermore, wealth and prosperity, technological advance, widespread education, democratic political forms, even honestly good intentions and avowals of good will have, by their failure to produce peace, brotherhood, serenity, and happiness, confronted us even more nakedly and unavoidably with the profundities that mankind has been avoiding by its busy-ness with the superficial.

[1] By A. H. Maslow. Copyright 1959 by Harper and Row.

82

We are reminded here of the "neurosis of success." People can struggle on hopefully, and even happily, for false panaceas so long as these are not attained. Once attained, however, they are soon discovered to be false hopes. Collapse and hopelessness ensue and continue until new hopes become possible.

We too are in an interregnum between old value systems that have not worked and new ones not yet born, an empty period which could be borne more patiently were it not for the great and unique dangers that beset mankind. We are faced with the real possibility of annihilation, and with the certainty of "small" wars, of racial hostilities, and of widespread exploitation. Specieshood is far in the future.

The cure for this disease is obvious. We need a validated, usable system of human values, values that we can believe in and devote ourselves to because they are true rather than because we are exhorted to "believe and have faith."

And for the first time in history, many of us feel, such a system—based squarely upon valid knowledge of the nature of man, of his society, and of his works—may be possible.

This is not to maintain that this knowledge is *now* available in the final form necessary for breeding conviction and action. It is not. What *is* available, however, is enough to give us confidence that we know the kinds of work that have to be done in order to progress toward such a goal. It appears possible for man, by his own philosophical and scientific efforts, to move toward self-improvement and social improvement.

❧ APPENDIX F ❧

RHAPSODIC, ISOMORPHIC
COMMUNICATIONS

In trying to elicit reports of peak-experiences from re-
luctant subjects or from non-peakers, I evolved a different
kind of interview procedure without being consciously
aware that I had done so. The "rhapsodic communication,"
as I have called it, consists of a kind of emotional con-
tagion in isomorphic parallel. It may have considerable
implications for both the theory of science and the philosophy of education.

Direct verbal description of peak-experiences in a sober,
cool, analytic, "scientific" way succeeds only with those
who already know what you mean, i.e., people who have
vivid peaks and who can, therefore, feel or intuit what you
are trying to point to even when your words are quite
inadequate in themselves.

As I went on interviewing, I "learned," without realizing
that I was learning, to shift over more and more to figures
of speech, metaphors, similes, etc., and, in general, to use
more and more poetic speech. It turns out that these are
often more apt to "click," to touch off an echoing experi-

ence, a parallel, isomorphic vibration than are sober, cool, carefully descriptive phrases.

We are taught here that the word "ineffable" means "not communicable by words that are analytic, abstract, linear, rational, exact, etc." Poetic and metaphorical language, physiognomic and synesthetic language, primary process language of the kind found in dreams, reveries, free associations and fantasies, not to mention pre-words and non-words such as gestures, tone of voice, style of speaking, body tonus, facial expressions—all these are more efficacious in communicating certain aspects of the ineffable.

This procedure can wind up being a kind of continuing rhapsodic, emotional, eager throwing out of one example after another of peaks, described or rather reported, expressed, shared, "celebrated," sung vividly with participation and with obvious approval and even joy. This kind of procedure can more often kindle into flame the latent or weak peak-experiences within the other person.

The problem here was not the usual one in teaching. It was not a labelling of something public that both could simultaneously see while the teacher pointed to it and named it. Rather it was trying to get the person to focus attention, to notice, to name an experience inside himself, which only he could feel, an experience, furthermore, which was not happening at the time. No pointing is possible here, no naming of something visible, no controlled and purposeful creation of the experience like turning on an electric current at will or probing at a painful spot.

In such an effort, one realizes vividly how isolated people's insides are from each other. It is as if two encapsulated privacies were trying to communicate with each other across the chasm between them. When the experience one is trying to communicate has no parallel in the other person, as in trying to describe color to the congenitally blind, then words fail almost (but not) entirely. If the other person turns out to be a literal non-peaker, then rhapsodic, isomorphic communication will not work.

In retrospect, I can see that I gradually began to assume that the non-speaker was a *weak* peaker rather than a person lacking the capacity altogether. I was, in effect, trying to fan his slumbering fire into open flame by my emotionally involved and approving accounts of other people's stronger experiences, as a tuning fork will set off a sympathetic piano wire across the room.

In effect, I proceeded "as if" I was trying to make a non-peaker into a peaker, or, better said, to make the self-styled non-peaker realize that he really was a peaker after all. I couldn't teach him how to have a peak-experience; but I could teach that he had already had it.

Whatever sensitizes the non-peaker to his own peaks will thereby make him *fertile ground for the seeds which the great peakers will cast upon him*. The great seers, prophets, or peakers may then be used as we now use artists, i.e., as people who are more sensitive, more reactive, who get a profounder, fuller, deeper peak-experience which then they can pass on to other people who are at least peakers enough to be able to be a good audience. Trying to teach the general population how to paint will certainly not make them into great painters, but it can very well make them into a better audience for great artists. Just as it is necessary to be a bit of an artist oneself before one can understand a great artist, so it is apparently necessary to become a small seer oneself before one can understand the great seers.

This is a kind of I-thou communication of intimates, of friends, of sweethearts, or of brothers rather than the more usual kind of subject-object, perceiver-percept, investigator-subject relationship in which separation, distance, detachment are thought to be the only way to bring greater objectivity.

Something of the sort has been discovered in other situations. For instance, in using psychedelic drugs to produce peak-experiences, general experience has been that if the atmosphere is coldly clinical or investigatory, and if the subject is watched and studied as if with a microscope, like a bug on a pin, then peaks are less apt to occur and unhappy experiences are more apt to occur. When the atmosphere becomes one of brotherly communion, however, with perhaps one of the "investigator-brothers" himself also taking the drug, then the experience is much more likely to be ecstatic and transcendent.

Something similar has been discovered by the Alcoholics Anonymous and by the Synanon groups for drug addicts. The person who has shared the experience can be brotherly and loving in a way that dispels the dominance hierarchy implied in the usual helping relationship. The reported reciprocal interdependence of performers and audiences could also serve as an example of this same kind of communication.

87

The existential and humanistic psychotherapists are also beginning to report that the "I-Thou encounter" can bring certain results which cannot be brought about by the classical Freudian mirror-type psychoanalyst (although I feel sure that the reverse is also true for certain *other* therapeutic results). Even the classical psychoanalysts would now be willing to admit, I think, that care, concern, and agapean love for the patient are implied, and *must* be implied, by the analyst in order that therapy may take place.

The ethologists have learned that if you want to study ducks and to learn all that is possible to know about ducks, then you had better love ducks. And so also, I believe, for stars, or numbers, or chemicals. This kind of love or interest or fascination is not contradictory of objectivity or truthfulness but is rather a precondition of certain kinds of objectivity, perspicuity, and receptivity. B-love encourages B-cognition, i.e., unselfish, understanding love for the Being or intrinsic nature of the other, makes it possible to perceive and to enjoy the other as an end in himself (not as a selfish means or as an instrument), and, therefore, makes more possible the perception of the nature of the other in its own right.

All (?), or very many, people, including even young children, can in principle be taught in some such experiential way that peak-experiences exist, what they are like, when they are apt to come, to whom they are apt to come, what will make them more likely, what their connection is with a good life, with a good man, with good psychological health, etc. To some extent, this can be done even with words, with lectures, with books. My experience has been that whenever I have lectured approvingly about peak-experiences, it was as if I had given permission to the peak-experiences of *some* people, at least, in my audience to come into consciousness. That is, even mere words sometimes seem to be able to remove the inhibitions, the blocks, and the fears, the rejections which had kept the peak-experiences hidden and suppressed.

All of this implies another *kind* of education, i.e., experiential education. But not only this, it also implies another kind of communication, the communication between alonenesses, between encapsulated, isolated egos. What we are implying is that in the kind of experiential teaching which is being discussed here, what is necessary to do first is to change the person and to change his awareness of himself. That is, what we must do is to make him become aware of the fact that peak-experiences go on inside himself. Until he has become aware of such experience and has this experience as a basis for comparison, he is a non-peaker; and it is useless to try to communicate to him the feel and the nature of peak-experience. But if we can change him, in the sense of making him aware of what is going on inside himself, then he becomes a different kind of communicatee. It is now possible to communicate with him. He now knows what you are talking about when you speak of peak-experiences; and it is possible to teach him by reference to his own weak peak-experiences how to improve them, how to enrich them, how to enlarge them, and also how to draw the proper conclusions from these experiences.

It can be pointed out that something of this kind goes

on normally in uncovering, insight psychotherapy. Part of the process here is an experiential-educational one in which we help the patient become aware of what he has been experiencing without having been aware of it. If we can teach him that such and such a constellation of pre-verbal subjective happenings has the label "anxiety," then thereafter it is possible to communicate with him about anxiety and all the conditions that bring it about, how to increase it, how to decrease it, etc. Until that point is reached at which he has a conscious, objective, detached awareness of the relationship between a particular name or label or word and a particular set of subjective, ineffable experiences, no communication and no teaching are possible; so also for passivity or hostility or yearning for love or whatever. In all of these, we may use the paradigm that the process of education (and of therapy) is helping the person to become aware of internal, subjective, subverbal experiences, so that these experiences can be brought into the world of abstraction, of conversation, of communication, of naming, etc., with the consequence that it immediately becomes possible for a certain amount of control to be exerted over these hitherto unconscious and uncontrollable processes.

One trouble with this kind of communication, for me at least, has been that I felt rhapsodizing to be artificial when I tried to do it deliberately and consciously. I became fully aware of what I had been doing only after trying to describe it in a conversation with Dr. David Nowlis. But since then I have not been able to communicate in the same way.

B-VALUES AS DESCRIPTIONS OF PERCEPTION IN PEAK-EXPERIENCES

The described characteristics of Being are also the values of Being. These Being-values are perceived as ultimate and as further unanalyzable (and yet they can each be defined in terms of each and all of the others). They are paralleled also by the characteristics of selfhood (identity) in peak-experiences; the characteristics of ideal art; the characteristics of ideal mathematical demonstrations; of ideal experiments and theories; of ideal science and knowledge; the far goals of all ideal, uncovering (Taoistic, non-interfering) psychotherapies; the far goals of the ideal humanistic education; the far goals and the expression of some kinds of religion; the characteristics of the ideally good environment and of the ideally good society (62).

The following may be seen either as a list of the described attributes of reality when perceived in peak-experiences, *or* as a list of the irreducible, intrinsic values of this reality.

1. Truth: honesty; reality; (nakedness; simplicity; richness; essentiality; oughtness; beauty; pure; clean and unadulterated completeness).

2. Goodness: (rightness; desirability; oughtness; justice; benevolence; honesty); (we love it, are attracted to it, approve of it).

3. Beauty: (rightness; form; aliveness; simplicity; richness; wholeness; perfection; completion; uniqueness; honesty).

4. Wholeness: (unity; integration; tendency to oneness; interconnectedness; simplicity; organization; structure; order; not dissociated; synergy; homonomous and integrative tendencies).

4a. Dichotomy-transcendence: (acceptance, resolution, integration, or transcendence of dichotomies, polarities, opposites, contradictions); synergy (i.e., transformation of oppositions into unities, of antagonists into collaborating or mutually enhancing partners).

5. Aliveness: (process; not-deadness; dynamic; eternal; flowing; self-perpetuating; spontaneity; self-moving energy; self-forming; self-regulation; full-functioning; changing and yet remaining the same; expressing itself; never-ending).

6. Uniqueness: (idiosyncrasy; individuality; singularity; non-comparability; its defining-characteristics; novelty; quale; suchness; nothing else like it).

7. Perfection: (nothing superfluous; nothing lacking; everything in its right place; unimprovable; just-

rightness; just-so-ness; suitability; justice; completeness; nothing beyond; oughtness).

7a. Necessity: (inevitability; it must be *just* that way;
not changed in any slightest way; and it is good that
it *is* that way).

8. Completion: (ending; finality; justice; it's finished;
no more changing of the Gestalt; fulfillment; *finis* and
telos; nothing missing or lacking; totality; fulfillment
of destiny; cessation; climax; consummation; closure; death before rebirth; cessation and completion
of growth and development; total gratification with
no more gratification possible; no striving; no movement toward any goal because already there; not
pointing to anything beyond itself).

9. Justice: (fairness; oughtness; suitability; architec-
tonic quality; necessity; inevitability; disinterested-
ness; non-partiality).

9a. Order: (lawfulness; rightness; rhythm; regularity;
symmetry; structure; nothing superfluous; perfectly
arranged).

10. Simplicity: (honesty; nakedness; purity; essentiality;
succinctness; [mathematical] elegance; abstract; un-
mistakability; essential skeletal structure; the heart
of the matter; bluntness; only that which is necessary;
without ornament, nothing extra or superfluous).

11. Richness: (totality; differentiation; complexity; in-
tricacy; nothing missing or hidden; all there; "non-
importance," i.e., everything is equally important;

93

nothing is unimportant; everything left the way
it is, without improving, simplifying, abstracting,
rearranging; comprehensiveness).

12. Effortlessness: (ease; lack of strain, striving, or difficulty; grace; perfect and beautiful functioning).

13. Playfulness: (fun; joy; amusement; gaiety; humor;
exuberance; effortlessness).

14. Self-sufficiency: (autonomy; independence; not needing anything other than itself in order to be itself;
self-determining; environment-transcendence; sepa-
rateness; living by its own laws; identity).

The descriptive B-values, seen as aspects of reality,
should be distinguished from the attitudes or emotions of
the B-cognizer *toward* this cognized reality and its attributes, e.g., awe, love, adoration, worship, humility, feeling of smallness plus godlikeness, reverence, approval of,
agreement with, wonder, sense of mystery, gratitude, devotion, dedication, identification with, belonging to, fusion
with, surprise and incredulousness, fear, joy, rapture, bliss,
ecstasy, etc.

One recurring problem for all organized, revealed religions during the last century has been the flat contradiction between their claim to final, total, unchangeable,
eternal and absolute truth and the cultural, historical, and
economic flux and relativism affirmed by the developing
social sciences and by the philosophers of science. Any
philosophy or religious system which has no place for flux
and for relativism is untenable (because it is untrue to

all the facts). But the human yearnings for peace, stability, for unity, for some kind of certainty, all continue to exist and to seek fulfillment even after the religious establishments have failed to do the job.

It may be that data from the peak-experiences will one day offer a possible resolution or transcendence of the dichotomy between relative and absolute, historical and eternal. The B-values derived from the peak-experiences, as well as from other sources (62), may supply us with a perfectly naturalistic variety of "certainty," of unity, of eternity, of universality. Of course, all these words will have to be understood in a particular way that is novel and unfamiliar. And yet, enough of the old, yearned-for meaning is retained to supply the fulfillment that the organized religions used to claim they could supply.

Of course, these "ultimate truths," if they are confirmed, are still truths within a system. That is, they seem to be true *for the human species.* That is, in the same sense that Euclidian theorems are absolutely true *within the Euclidian system.* Again, just as Euclidian propositions are ultimately tautologous, so also the B-values (See Appendix F) may very well turn out to be defining characteristics of humanness in its essence, i.e., *sine qua non* aspects of the concept "human," and, therefore, tautologous. The statement, "The fully human person in certain moments perceives the unity of the cosmos, fuses with it, and rests in it, completely satisfied for the moment in his yearning for one-ness," is very likely synonymous, at a "higher level of magnification" (59), with the statement, "This is a fully human person."

95

For the moment, I shan't attempt to go beyond these "species-relative absolutes" to discuss the absolutes that would remain if the human species were to disappear. It is sufficient at this point to affirm that the B-values *are* absolutes of a kind, a humanly satisfying kind, which, furthermore, are "cosmocentric" in Marcel's sense, and not personally relative or selfishly ego-centered.

🌿 Appendix H 🌿

NATURALISTIC REASONS FOR PREFERRING GROWTH-VALUES OVER REGRESSION-VALUES UNDER GOOD CONDITIONS

Descriptively, we can see in each person his own (weak) tendencies to grow toward self-actualization; and also descriptively, we can see his various (weak) tendencies toward regressing (out of fear, hostility, or laziness). It is the task of education, therapy, marriage, and the family to ally themselves to the former, and to be conducive to individual growth. But why? How to prove this? Why is this not just a covert smuggling in of the arbitrary, concealed values of the therapist?

1. Clinical experience and also some experimental evidence teaches us that the consequences of making growth-choices are "better" in terms of the person's own biological values, e.g., physical health; absence of pain, discomfort, anxiety, tension, insomnia, nightmares, indigestion, constipation, etc.; longevity, lack of fear, pleasure in fully-functioning; beauty, sexual prowess, sexual attractiveness, good teeth, good hair, good feet, etc.; good pregnancy, good birth, good death; more fun, more pleasure, more

happiness, more peak-experiences, etc. That is, if a person could himself see all the likely consequences of growth and all the likely consequences of coasting or of regression, and if he were allowed to choose between them, he would always (in principle, and under "good conditions") choose the consequences of growth and reject the consequences of regression. That is, the more one knows of the actual consequences of growth-choices and regression-choices, the more attractive become the growth-choices to practically any human being. And these are the actual choices he is prone to make if conditions are good, i.e., if he is allowed truly free choice so that his organism can express its own nature.

2. The consequences of making growth-choices are more in accordance with paradic design (C. Daly King), with actual use of the capacities (instead of inhibition, atophy, or diminution), i.e., with using the joints, the muscles, the brain, the genitalia, etc., instead of not using them, or using them in a conflicted or inefficient fashion, or in losing the use of them.

3. The consequences of growth are more in accordance with either Darwin-type survival and expansion or with Kropotkin-type survival and expansion. That is, growth has more survival value than regression and defense (under "good" conditions). (Regression and defense sometimes have more survival value for a particular individual under "bad" conditions, i.e., when there is not enough to go around, not enough need gratifiers, conditions of mutually exclusive interests, of hostility, divisiveness, etc. But "bad" conditions always means that this greater sur-

vival value for some must be paid for by lesser survival value for others. The greater survival value for the individual under "good" conditions, however, is "free," i.e., it doesn't cost anybody anything.)

4. Growth is more in accordance with fulfilling Hartman's definition (27) of the "good" human being. That is, it is a better way of achieving more of the defining characteristics of the concept "human being." Regression and defense, living at the safety level, is a way of giving up many of these "higher" defining characteristics for the sake of sheer survival. ("Bad" conditions can also be defined circularly as conditions which make lower-need gratifications possible only at the cost of giving up higher-need gratifications.)

5. The foregoing paragraph can be phrased in a somewhat different way, generating different problems and a different vocabulary. We can begin with selecting out the "best specimen," the exemplar, the "type specimen" of the taxonomists, i.e., the most fully developed and most fully "characteristic" of those characteristics which define the species (e.g., the most tigerish tiger, the most leonine lion, the most canine dog, etc.), in the same way that is now done at 4-H meetings where the healthiest young man or woman is selected out. If we use this "best specimen," in the zookeeper or taxonomist sense, as a model, then growth conduces to moving toward becoming like this model, and regression moves away from it.

6. It looks as if the non-pathological baby put into free-choice situations, with plenty of choice, tends to choose its way toward growth rather than toward regression

(61). In the same way, a plant or an animal selects from the millions of objects in the world those which are "right" for its nature. This is based on its own physical-chemical-biological nature, e.g., what the rootlets will let through and what they won't, what can be metabolized and what cannot, what can be digested and what cannot, whether sunshine or rain helps or hurts, etc.

7. Very important as a source of data to support the biological basis of choosing growth over regression is the experience with "uncovering therapy" or what I have begun to call Taoistic therapy. What emerges here is the person's own nature, his own identity, his bent, his own tastes, his vocation, his species values, and his idiosyncratic values. These idiosyncratic values are so often different from the idiosyncratic values of the therapist as to constitute a validation of the point, i.e., uncovering therapy is truly uncovering rather than indoctrination (48).

The conditions which make uncovering likely have been well spelled out, e.g., by Rogers (82), and are included in our more general and more inclusive conception of "good conditions."

"Good conditions" can be defined in terms of a good free-choice situation. Everything is there that the organism might need or choose or prefer. There is no external constraint to choose one action or thing rather than another. The organism has not already had a choice built in from past habituation, familiarization, negative or positive conditionings or reinforcements, or extrinsic and (biologically) arbitrary cultural evaluations. There is no extrinsic reward or punishment for making one choice rather than another. There is plenty of everything. Certain technical conditions of really free choice are fulfilled: the items from among which the choice is to be made are spatially and temporally contiguous, enough time is permitted, etc.

In other words, "good conditions" means mostly (entirely?) good conditions for permitting truly free choice by the organism. This means that good conditions permit the intrinsic, instinctoid nature of the organism to show itself by its preferences. *It* tells us what it prefers, and we now assume these preferences to express its needs, i.e., all that which is necessary for the organism to be itself, and to prevent it from becoming less than itself (61).

Although the above is mostly true, it is not altogether so. For one thing, it has been discovered in several species that there are "good choosers" and "bad choosers"; and it may be that this is constitutionally based, not only among non-human animals, but also among human babies. A few babies cannot choose well in the free-choice situation, i.e., they sicken. Secondly, this free-choice "wisdom" is easily destroyed in the human being by previous habituation, cultural conditioning, neurosis, physical illnesses, etc. etc.

Thirdly, and perhaps most important, is that human children do *not* choose discipline, restraint, delay, frustration, even where this is "good for them." Free choice "wisdom" seems to work only or mostly as of the immediate moment. It is a response to the present field or current situation. It does not prepare well for the future. The child is "now-bound"; and while this may be no handicap in a very simple, preliterate society, it is a terrible handicap in a technologically advanced society. Therefore, the greater intelligence, knowledge, and foreknowledge of the adult is necessary as a control upon the child. Human beings need each other far more for the early stages of growth than any other species. We should also mention here Goldstein's important point (23) that children who are not yet able to abstract can function only because adults are available to abstract for them.

This implies that the definition of "good conditions" for human beings has characteristics in addition to those generalized ones listed above, e.g., availability of benevolent elders to be dependent upon, and (in a complex society) plenty of brotherly others who can be counted on to do their part in the division of labor.

Finally, because human beings have "higher needs" in addition to the "lower needs" they share with other animals and since these needs, e.g., for safety, belongingness, love, respect, all are satisfiable only by other human beings, then a free-choice situation must include these higher-need gratifications. This, in turn, brings up the whole question of the nature of the mother, of the family, of the subculture, and of the larger culture. "Good cultural conditions" may be defined in terms of the same requirement (of the free-choice situation) that we have already used, i.e., the "good culture" must supply the higher-need gratifications as well as the lower-need gratifications. With this enrichment of the definition clearly kept in mind, it is not necessary to change the description above, although it *is* necessary to develop a comparative sociology of healthy and rich cultures in order to understand fully all the social implications of the definition (69).

AN EXAMPLE OF B-ANALYSIS

Any woman can be seen under the aspect of eternity, in her capacity as a symbol, as a goddess, priestess, sibyl, as mother earth, as the eternal flowing breasts, as the uterus from which life comes, and as the life-giver, the life-creator. This can also be seen operationally in terms of the Jungian archetypes which can be recovered in several ways. I have managed to get it in good introspectors simply by asking them directly to free associate to a particular symbol. The psychoanalytic literature, of course, has many such reports. Practically every deep case history will report such symbolic, archaic ways of viewing the woman, both in her good aspects and her bad aspects. (Both the Jungians and the Kleinians recognize the great and good mother and the witch mother as basic archetypes.) Another way of getting at this is in terms of the artificial dream that is suggested under hypnosis. It can also probably be investigated by spontaneous drawings, as the art therapists have pointed out. Still another possibility is the George Klein technique of two cards very rapidly succeeding each other so that symbolism can be studied. Any person who has been psychoanalyzed can fairly easily fall into such symbolic or metaphorical thinking in his dreams or free associations or fantasies or reveries. It is possible then to see the woman under the aspect of her Being. Another way of saying this is that she is to be seen in her sacred, rather than the profane, aspects; or under the holy or pious aspects; or from the point of view of eternity or infinity; from the point of view of perfection; from the point of view of the ideal end-goal; from the point of view of what in principle any woman could have become. This fits in with the self-actualization theory that any new-born baby in principle has the capacity to become perfect or healthy or virtuous although we know very well that in actuality most of them won't.

On the other hand, the woman seen in her D-aspect, in the world of deficiencies, of worries and bills and anxieties and wars and fears and pains, is profane rather than sacred, momentary rather than eternal, local rather than infinite, etc. Here we see in women what is equally true: they can be bitches, selfish, empty-headed, stupid, foolish, catty, trivial, boring, mean, whorish. The D-aspect and B-aspect are equally true.

The general point is: we must try to see *both* or else bad things can happen psychologically. For one thing, if the woman is seen *only* as a goddess, as the madonna, as unearthly beauty, as on a pedestal, as in the sky or in Heaven, then she becomes inaccessible to the male—she can't be played with or made love to. She isn't earthy or fleshy enough. In the critical situations in which this actually happens with men, i.e., where they identify women with the madonna or with the mother, they often become sexually impotent and find it impossible to have sexual intercourse with such a woman. This is good neither for his pleasure nor for her pleasure either, especially since making madonnas out of some women is apt to go along with making prostitutes out of other women. And then the whole madonna-prostitute complex which is so familiar to the clinician comes up, in which sex is impossible with good and noble and perfect women, but is possible only with dirty or nasty or low women. Somehow it is necessary to be able to see the B-woman, the actually noble and wonderful goddess-woman, and also the D-woman, who sometimes sweats and stinks and who gets belly aches, and with whom one can go to bed.

On the other hand, we have very considerable clinical information about what happens when men can see women only in their D-aspect and are unable to see them as beautiful and noble and virtuous and wonderful as well. This breeds what Kirkendall in his book on sex has called the exploitative relationship. It can get very ugly both for men and for women and can deprive them both of the really great pleasures of life. Certainly it can deprive them of all the love pleasures, which means also most of the major sex pleasures (because the people who can't love don't get the same kind of thrill out of sex as the people who can love and who can get romantic). The men who think of women merely as sexual objects and who call them by purely sexual names—thereby depersonalize the woman as if she were not person enough to be called a human being. This is obviously bad for her—but in a more subtle way it is also very bad for him, in the sense that every exploiter is damaged by being an exploiter. The possibility of being friends across such exploitative lines is practically zero, which means that men and women, the two halves of the human species, are cut off from one another. They can never learn the delights of being fused with each other, of being friendly, affectionate, loving partners, or the like. To sum this up, it means that there are horrors in seeing the woman only in the B-way, and there are horrors in seeing her only in a D-way, and clearly the psychologically healthy goal is for these to be combined or to alternate or to be fused in some way.

It is this fusion that I can use as an example of the more general problem of fusing the B-psychology and the D-psychology, the sacred and the profane, the eternal and the temporal, the infinite and the local, the perfect and the defective, and so on.

Seeing the man in a B-way means seeing also his ultimate, ideal possibilities, in Marion Milner's case, as God the Father, as all-powerful, as the one who created the world and who rules the world of things, the world outside, the world of nature, and who changes it and masters it and conquers it. Also at this deep level, Milner, and probably many other women, will identify the noble man, the B-man, as the spirit of rationality, the spirit of intelligence, of probing and exploring, of mathematics, and the like. The male as a father image is strong and capable, fearless, noble, clean, not trivial, not small, a protector of the weak, the innocent, children and orphans and widows, the hunter and bringer of food, and so on. Secondly, he can be seen archaically as the master and the conqueror of nature, the engineer, the carpenter, the builder, which the woman is generally not. It is quite probable that women, when they get into the eternal mood, or into the B-attitude, must see men in this ideal way even if they can't see their own particular man in this way. The very fact that a woman is dissatisfied with her own man may be an indication that she has some other image or imago or ideal in mind to which he doesn't measure up. I think that investigation would show that this ideal was as Milner expressed it and as it is seen also in the direct investigations of schizophrenics of the sort that John Rosen did. Clearly any woman who could not see her man (or some man anyhow) in this way could not use men, would have to disrespect them, might need a man in the D-world, but deep down would be contemptuous because he didn't measure up to the B-realm.

(I should mention that we already have a kind of precursor, a model of the B-woman and the B-man in the child's attitude toward his mother and father. Through his eyes they can be seen as perfect and godlike and so on. This attitude can be retained by any child who has the good fortune of having a good enough mother and a good enough father so as to permit such attitudes to be formed, i.e., to give him some notion of what the ideally good woman and of what the ideally good man could be.)

The D-man, in the world of trivialities, the world of striving, etc. may not be able to induce the B-attitude in his woman, but this seems to be a necessity if she is to be able to love a man fully. At this deep level, it's necessary for her to be able to adore a man, to look up to him as once she looked up to her father, to be able to lean on him, to be able to trust him, to feel him to be reliable, to feel him to be strong enough so that she can feel precious, delicate, dainty, and so that she can trustfully snuggle down on his lap and let him take care of her and the babies, and the world, and everything else outside the home. This is especially so when she's pregnant, or when she's raising small infants and children. Then she most needs a man around to take care of her, to protect her, and to mediate between her and the world, to go out and hunt the deer and get the food, to chop the wood, and so on. If she cannot see her man (or *any* man) in a B-way, then such looking up to, respect, adoration, perhaps surrender, giving in to him, fearing him a bit, trying to please him, loving him, all of this becomes in principle impossible. She may make a good arrangement with him, but at a very profound level she will be deprived. If she cannot perceive in him the ultimate, eternal, B-masculine qualities, either because he hasn't got enough of them or because she is incapable of perceiving in a B-way (either one can happen), then, in effect, she has no man at all. She may have a boy, a son, a child, a neuter of some sort, a hermaphrodite, but she has no man in the ultimate sense. Therefore, she must be profoundly and deeply unhappy as any woman without a man must be. In the same way, any man without a woman in the B-sense must be profoundly unhappy, stunted, missing something, deprived of a very basic experience, a basic richness in life.

If the woman (like the prostitutes and call girls that the

psychoanalysts have been writing about recently) can have toward men only a D-attitude (because of the defects in their own relations with their fathers), then such women have a hopeless future so far as happiness is concerned. In the same way, the D-men who see women only in a D-way can have only a half-life. The D-woman or the woman who can see men only in a D-way can have no relationship to a man except to exploit him, and this will make for the expected consequences of enmity and hatred across the sex lines.

If the woman can see her man *only* as B-man, then she too can't sleep with him, or at least not be able to enjoy him sexually, because this would be like sleeping with her own father or a god, etc. He must be sufficiently down to earth so that she isn't too awed by him. He must be homey, so to speak, part of the actual world and not some ethereal, angelic figure who will never have an erection and who won't have sexual impulses, etc. I may say also that a woman whose strong impulse is to see man, her man, only in the B-way is shocked every time such a man behaves in the normal, natural, human, everyday D-way, i.e., if he goes to the toilet, if he shows himself to have faults, or if he's not perfect. Since she is apt to be horrified, shocked, disillusioned, and disappointed by his D-behavior, this means that she can never live with any man (*any* man would shock her and disillusion her, because no man is *only* a B-man).

The good man, the most desirable we know, is a combination of the B and the D. The same is true for the good woman who is a combination of the B and the D. She must be able to be a madonna, partly; she must be able to be motherly; she must be able to be holy; she must be able to strike awe into the heart of the man, at times; but also, she must come down to earth, and he must be able to see her come down to earth without getting shocked. The truth is she also goes to the toilet, and she also sweats and also has belly aches and gets fat and so on. She is of the earth; and if he has any need to make her of the sky only, then trouble is inevitable.

Now the truth is that any woman, especially to the perceptive eye, to the sensitive man, to the more aesthetic man, to the more intelligent man, to the more healthy man, can be seen in a B-way, with B-cognition, however horrible or dirty or ugly or bitchy or however much a prostitute or a psychopath or a gold digger or a hateful murderess or a witch she may be. The truth is that at some moments she will suddenly flip into her goddess-like aspect, most especially when she's fulfilling those biological functions that men see as basically female: nursing, feeding, giving birth, taking care of children, cleaning the baby, being beautiful, being sexually exciting, etc. It would take a pretty stunted and diminished man not to be able to see this ever. (Can a man who is reduced to the concrete see a woman in a B-way?) The man who is conscious only of the D-characteristics of women is not living the unitive life, is not seeing Heaven on earth, is not seeing the eternal characteristics which exist all around him. To put it bluntly, such a man is being blind to certain aspects of the real world.

This kind of analysis should teach people to see *gen-*

erally in a more unitive or B-cognitive fashion. Not only should men see the B-aspects of women, but women themselves should occasionally feel their own B-aspects, i.e., they should feel like priestesses at certain moments, feel symbolic as they give the breast to the baby, or nurse the wounded soldier, or bake bread. Once we become fully conscious of this twofold nature of people, we should more often see a woman setting out dinner on the table for her family as going through some kind of ritual or ceremony like a ritual or ceremonial dance in some religious place (ritual in the very strict sense that she is not only shoving a lamb chop into his mouth or feeding his gut but is re-enacting, in a dramatic fashion, in a symbolic fashion, in a poetic fashion, the eternal relation between man and woman). Symbolically this is almost as if she were giving her husband the breast out of which comes milk and food and life and nourishment. It can be seen in this way, and she can take on the noble proportions of a priestess in some ancient religion.

So also, with this sensitizing, should it become possible for us to see the man coming home with his pay check as acting out an ancient ritual of bringing home a food animal that he has killed in a hunt and that he tosses down with a lordly air for his wife and children and dependents, while they look on with admiration because they can't do it and he can. Now it certainly is true that it is harder to see the B-man in this aspect of hunter and provider in a man who is actually a bookkeeper in an office with three thousand other bookkeepers. Yet the fact remains that he can be seen so and should be. So also for the awesome way in which he willingly takes on his shoulders the responsibility for supporting his family; this too can be seen in a B-way, as an ancient and holy act. The right kind of education may actually help women to realize these basic, symbolic, archaic, ritual, ceremonial aspects of their husbands and make the husband also feel a slightly pious or holy thrill as he goes through the ancient ritual of entering his wife sexually, or of taking food from her, or of having her disrobe before him freely, or of being awestruck and pious and worshipful as he comes into the hospital where she has just delivered a baby, or perhaps even with the ceremony of menstruation. To pay a bill with money that he has earned, perhaps in some unexciting way, e.g., selling shoes, is actually in a straight biological line with the cavemen and their caring for their families.

Rather than being a local and temporary nuisance, menstruation can be seen as a biological drama that has to do with the very profound biological rhythm of reproduction and life and death. Each menstruation, after all, represents a baby that could have been. This may be seen strictly as a mystery by the man because it is something he doesn't experience, something he doesn't know about, something which is altogether woman's secret. Menstruation has been called the weeping of a disappointed uterus; this puts it squarely in the B-realm, and makes of it a holy ceremony rather than a messy accident or "curse."

For practically all primitives, these matters that I have spoken about are seen in a more pious, sacred way, as Eliade has stressed, i.e., as rituals, ceremonies, and mysteries. The ceremony of puberty, which we make nothing of, is extremely important for most primitive cultures. When the girl menstruates for the first time and becomes a woman, it is truly a great event and a great ceremony; and it is truly, in the profound and naturalistic and human sense, a great religious moment in the life not only of the girl herself but also of the whole tribe. She steps into the realm of those who can carry on life and those who can produce life; so also for the boy's puberty; so also for the ceremonies of death, of old age, of marriage, of the mysteries of women, the mysteries of men. I think that an examination of primitive or preliterate cultures would show that they often manage the unitive life better than we do, at least as far as relations between the sexes are concerned and also as between adults and children. They combine better than we do the B and the D, as Eliade has pointed out. He defined primitive cultures as different from industrial cultures because they have kept their sense of the sacred about the basic biological things of life.

We must remember, after all, that all these happenings are in truth mysteries. Even though they happen a million times, they are still mysteries. If we lose our sense of the mysterious, or the numinous, if we lose our sense of awe, of humility, of being struck dumb, if we lose our sense of good fortune, then we have lost a very real and basic human capacity and are diminished thereby.

Perceiving in this way can also be a powerful self-therapy. Again the truth of the matter is that any woman, any girl, any man, any boy, any child, is in *fact* a mysterious, wonderful, ceremonial, and ritual B-object. Practically every simple culture makes a big fuss over the woman

113

and her childbearing function and everything that has any-thing to do with it. Now, of course, their ceremonies over the placenta, the umbilical cord, or menstrual blood, and their various cleansing ceremonies may look ridiculous and superstitious to us. Yet the fact remains that they keep the whole area mythological (archaic, poetic, symbolic); by these methods, they keep it all sacred. Even where the woman is severely disadvantaged by, e.g., menstrual huts —where every menstruating woman must hide from all human contacts for a whole week, and must then take ritual baths, etc.—perhaps even this has certain advantages over just taking the whole matter for granted. Such a woman must think that her menstruation and her menstrual blood can be powerful and dangerous. She must, therefore, think of herself as a pretty powerful person who is capable of being dangerous. She matters, she's important. My guess is that this does something for her self-esteem as a woman. (I remember James Thurber's very funny and yet very touching cartoon, uncaptioned, of a lady with four cute children strung out behind her, meeting a dog with four cute puppies strung out behind her. The two mothers are caught turning back to look each other in the eye, sympa-thetically, with understanding, with fellow feeling, like two sisters.)

The same thing could be true for the man also, if all his mysteries were taken as true mysteries, e.g., the fact that he can produce erections and ejaculate spermatazoa, that these live, that they swim, that in some mysterious way they can penetrate the ovum and make a baby to grow, etc., etc. There are many myths in which the man in sexual intercourse with his wife is seen as a farmer, as a man with a plow, or as a man who is sowing seeds, or as a man who puts something into the earth. His ejaculation is not then just some casual spilling out of something: it becomes as much a ceremony, a mysterious, awe-inspiring, piety-producing ceremony as any high religious ceremony like the Mass, the Sun Dance, etc. Similarly, it might be desirable if we could teach our young men to think of their penises, for instance, as phallic worshipers do, as beautiful and holy objects, as awe inspiring, as mysterious, as big and strong, possibly dangerous and fear inspiring, as miracles which are not understood. If we can teach our young men this, not to mention our young women, then every boy will become the bearer of a holy thing, of a sceptre, of something given to him by nature which no woman can ever have. We supply him thereby with an ultimate and irreducible self-esteem which is his simply by virtue of being a male, a man with a penis and testicles, which should at times awe the woman and the man himself as well. This B-attitude should help him to maintain a sense of the holy or the sacred whenever he has an ejaculation, and should help him to think of his orgasm in the same way that the Tantrists and other religious sects do, i.e., as a unifying experience, a holy experience, a symbol, as a miracle, and as a religious ceremony.

Any woman who is at all sensitive to the philosophical must occasionally be awed by the great storms of sexuality that she can arouse in her man, and also by her power to allay and quiet these storms. This can be seen as goddess-like power, and therefore may be used as one basis for her profound biological self-esteem as a woman. Something similar can be true for male self-esteem, to the extent that he is able to arouse and to calm sexual storms in his wife.

Such perceptions and awarenesses should be able to help any male and any female to experience the transcendent and unitive, both in oneself and in the other. In this way, the eternal becomes visible *in* and *through* the particular, the symbolic and platonic can be experienced *in* and *through* the concrete instance, the sacred can fuse with the profane, and one can transcend the universe of time and space while being of it.

❧ BIBLIOGRAPHY ❧

1. Allen, R.; Haupt, T.; and Jones, R. "Analysis of Peak-Experiences Reported by Students," *Journal of Clinical Psychology,* 1964, **XX**, 207-212.

2. Allport, G. *Becoming.* New Haven, Conn.: Yale University Press, 1955.

3. ————. *The Individual and His Religion.* New York: Macmillan Co., 1950.

4. ————. *Pattern and Growth in Personality.* New York: Holt, Rinehart & Winston, Inc., 1961.

5. Angyal, A. Unpublished notes on psychotherapy and religion.

6. Baumer, F. L. *Religion and the Rise of Skepticism.* New York: Harcourt, Brace & Co., 1960.

7. Bertocci, P., and Millard, R. *Personality and the Good.* New York: David McKay Co., Inc., 1963.

8. Boisen, A. *The Exploration of the Inner World.* New York: Harper & Row, 1962.

9. Bonner, H. *Psychology of Personality.* New York: Ronald Press Co., 1961.

10. Bucke, R. *Cosmic Consciousness.* New York: E. P. Dutton & Co., Inc., 1923.

11. Bühler, C. *Values in Psychotherapy.* New York: Free Press of Glencoe, Inc., 1962.

117

12. Coleman, J. *Personality Dynamics and Effective Behavior*. Chicago: Scott, Foresman & Co., 1960.

13. Combs, A. (ed.). *Perceiving, Behaving, Becoming: A New Focus for Education*. Washington, D. C.: Association for Supervision and Curriculum Development, 1962.

14. Dewey, J. *A Common Faith*. New Haven, Conn.: Yale University Press, 1934.

15. Eliade, M. *The Sacred and the Profane*. New York: Harper & Bros., 1961.

16. "An Essential of Religion," *Manas*, Vol. XVI (February 13, 1963).

17. Frankl, V. *From Death Camp to Existentialism*. Boston: Beacon Press, 1963.

18. Freud, S. *Collected Papers*, 4 vols. London: Hogarth Press, Ltd., 1956.

19. ———. *The Future of an Illusion*. New York: Liveright Publishing Corp., 1949.

20. Fromm, E. *Man for Himself*. New York: Rinehart & Co., Inc., 1947.

21. ———. *Psychoanalysis and Religion*. New Haven, Conn.: Yale University Press, 1950.

22. ———; Suzuki, D. T.; and DeMartino, R. *Zen Buddhism and Psychoanalysis*. New York: Harper & Bros., 1961.

23. Goldstein, K. *Human Nature*. New York: Shocken Books, 1963.

24. ———. *The Organism*. Boston: Beacon Press, 1963.

25. Goodenough, E. R. *Toward a Mature Faith*. New Haven, Conn.: Yale University Press, 1955.

26. Halmos, P. *Towards a Measure of Man*. London: Kegan Paul, 1957.

27. Hartman, R. "The Science of Value," in *New Knowledge in Human Values*, ed. A. H. Maslow. New York: Harper & Bros., 1959.

28. Hartmann, H. *Psychoanalysis and Moral Values.* New York: International Universities Press, Inc., 1960.

29. Horney, K. *Neurosis and Human Growth.* New York: W. W. Norton & Co., Inc., 1950.

30. Huxley, A. *The Perennial Philosophy.* New York: Harper & Bros., 1944.

31. Huxley, J. *Religion Without Revelation.* New York: Mentor Books, 1958.

32. James, W. *Varieties of Religious Experience.* New York: Modern Library, Inc.

33. Johnson, R. L. *Watcher on the Hills.* New York: Harper & Bros., 1959.

34. Jourard, S. *Personal Adjustment.* Rev. ed. New York: Macmillan Co., 1963.

35. Jung, C. G. *Memories, Dreams, Reflections.* London: Collins, Routledge & Kegan Paul, Ltd., 1963.

36. ———. *Modern Man in Search of a Soul.* New York: Harcourt, Brace & Co., 1933.

37. ———. *Psychology and Religion.* New Haven, Conn.: Yale University Press, 1938.

38. King, C. D. "The Meaning of Normal," *Yale Journal of Biology and Medicine,* XVII (1945), 493-501.

39. Koestler, A. *The Lotus and the Robot.* London: Hutchinson & Co., Ltd., 1960.

40. Krutch, J. W. *Human Nature and the Human Condition.* New York: Random House, 1959.

41. ———. *The Measure of Man.* New York: Bobbs-Merrill Co., 1954.

42. Laski, M. *Ecstasy.* London: Cresset Press, Ltd., 1961.

43. LeShan, L., and LeShan, E. "Psychotherapy and the Patient with a Limited Life Span," *Psychiatry,* XXIV (1961), 318-23.

44. MacLeod, R. *Religious Perspectives of College Teaching in Experimental Psychology*. New Haven, Conn.: Edward W. Hazen Foundation, 1952.

45. Manual, F. *The Eighteenth Century Confronts the Gods*. Cambridge, Mass.: Harvard University Press, 1959.

46. Maslow, A. H. "The Authoritarian Character Structure," *Journal of Social Psychology*, XVIII (1943), 401-411.

47. ———. "Comments on Skinner's Attitude to Science," *Daedalus*, XC (1961), 572-73.

48. ———. "Isomorphic Interrelations between Knower and Known," in *Sign, Image, Symbol*, ed. G. Kepes. New York: George Braziller, Inc., 1966.

49. ———. "The Creative Attitude," *The Structurist*, No. 3 (1963), pp. 4-10.

50. ———. "Criteria for Judging Needs To Be Instinctoid," *Proceedings of the International Congress of Psychology*, 1963.

51. ———. "Emotional Blocks to Creativity," *Journal of Individual Psychology*, XIV (1958), 51-56.

52. ———. "Eupsychia—The Good Society," *Journal of Humanistic Psychology*, I (1961), 1-11.

53. ———. "Further Notes on Being-Psychology," *Journal of Humanistic Psychology*, III (1963), 120-35.

54. ———. "Fusions of Facts and Values," *American Journal of Psychoanalysis*, XXIII (1963), 117-31.

55. ———. "The Influence of Familiarization on Preferences," *Journal of Experimental Psychology*, XXI (1937), 162-80.

56. ———, and Diaz-Guerrero, R. "Juvenile Delinquency as a Value Disturbance," in *Festschrift for Gardner Murphy*, ed. J. Peatman and E. Hartley. New York: Harper & Bros., 1960.

57. ———. "Lessons from the Peak-Experiences," *Journal of Humanistic Psychology*, II (1962), 9-18.

58. ———. "Mental Health and Religion," in *Religion, Science and Mental Health*. New York: New York University Press

for the Academy of Religion and Mental Health, 1959.

59. ———. *Motivation and Personality.* New York: Harper & Bros., 1954, 2nd ed., 1970.

60. ———. "The Need To Know and the Fear of Knowing," *Journal of General Psychology,* LXVIII (1963), 111-25.

61. ——— (ed.). *New Knowledge in Human Values.* New York: Harper & Bros., 1959.

62. ———. "Notes on Being-Psychology," *Journal of Humanistic Psychology,* II (1962), 47-71.

63. ———. "Notes on Innocent Cognition," in *Gegenswartsprobleme der Entwicklungspsychologie: Festschrift für Charlotte Bühler,* ed. H. Thomae. Göttingen: Verlag für Psychologie, 1963.

64. ———. "A Philosophy of Psychology," *Main Currents,* XIII (1956), 27-32.

65. ———. "Power Relationships and Patterns of Personal Development," in *Problems of Power in American Democracy,* ed. A. Kornhauser. Detroit: Wayne State University Press, 1957.

66. ———. "The Scientific Study of Values," *Proceedings of the 7th Congress of Inter-American Society of Psychology.* Mexico City, 1963.

67. ———. "Some Frontier Problems in Mental Health," in *Personality Theory and Counseling Practice,* ed. A. Combs. Gainesville, Fla.: University of Florida Press, 1961.

68. ———; Rand, H.; and Newman, S. "Some Parallels between the Dominance and Sexual Behavior of Monkeys and the Fantasies of Patients in Psychotherapy," *Journal of Nervous and Mental Disease,* CXXXI (1960), 202-212.

69. ———. *Eupsychian Management: A Journal.* Homewood, Ill.: Irwin-Dorsey, 1965.

70. ———. *Toward a Psychology of Being.* Princeton, N. J.: D. Van Nostrand Co., Inc., 1962, 2nd ed., 1968.

71. ———. "Two Kinds of Cognition and Their Integration," *General Semantics Bulletin*, Nos. 20, 21 (1957), 17-22.

72. May, R. (ed.). *Existential Psychology*. New York: Random House, 1961.

73. Mowrer, O. H. *The Crisis in Psychiatry and Religion*. Princeton, N. J.: D. Van Nostrand Co., Inc., 1961.

74. Mumford, L. *The Transformations of Man*. New York: Harper & Bros., 1956.

75. Murphy, G. *Human Potentialities*. New York: Basic Books, Inc., 1958.

76. Nowlis, D. "The Phenomenology of Transcendence." Unpublished Ph. D. dissertation, Harvard University, 1963.

77. Oates, W. *What Psychology Says about Religion*. New York: Association Press, 1958.

78. Otto, R. *The Idea of the Holy*. New York: Oxford University Press, 1958.

79. Pratt. J. B. *Eternal Values in Religion*. New York: Macmillan Co., 1950.

80. Progoff, I. *The Death and Rebirth of Psychology*. New York: Julian Press, Inc., 1956.

81. Rank, O. *Beyond Psychology*. Scranton, Pa.: Haddon Craftsmen, Inc., 1941.

82. Rogers, C. *On Becoming a Person*. Boston: Houghton Mifflin Co., 1961.

83. Thorne, F. C. "The Clinical Use of Peak and Nadir Experience Reports," *Journal of Clinical Psychology*, XIX (1963), 248-50.

84. Tillich, P. *The Courage To Be*. New Haven, Conn.: Yale University Press, 1952.

85. Toynbee, A. *A Study of History*. Vol. XII. New York: Oxford University Press, 1961.

86. Vogt, V. O. *Art and Religion*. Boston: Beacon Press, 1960.

87. Warmoth, A. "A Note on the Peak Experience as a Personal Myth," *Journal of Humanistic Psychology*, 1965, V, 18-21.

88. ———. "The Peak Experience and the Life History," *Journal of Humanistic Psychology*, III (1963), 86-91.

89. Wheelis, A. *The Quest for Identity*. New York: W. W. Norton & Co., Inc., 1958.

90. Wilson, C. *Religion and the Rebel*. Boston: Houghton Mifflin Co., 1957.

91. ———. *The Stature of Man*. Boston: Houghton Mifflin Co., 1959.

92. Zinker, J. "Rosa Lee: Motivation and the Crisis of Dying." Lake Erie College Studies. Painesville, Ohio: Lake Erie College Press, 1966.